PAVILION LIVING

Architecture, Patronage, and Well-Being

Victor Deupi

PAVILION LIVING

Architecture, Patronage, and Well-Being

Victor Deupi

Foreword by Peter Zimmerman
Preface by Julieann Shanahan
Principal Photography by Jeffrey Totaro
Edited by Oscar Riera Ojeda

OSCAR RIERA OJEDA
PUBLISHERS

To my father, John 'Jack' Kelly, who filled my
childhood with memories of Philadelphia.
Julieann

To my mother-in-law, Carol 'Nonna' Johnson,
a true lover of Pennsylvania field stone.
Victor

Table of Contents

Foreword
by Peter Zimmerman

— 22

Preface
by Julieann Shanahan

— 28

Introduction
Butterflies, Tents, and Wooden Shacks, a Brief History of Pavilions

— 40

Chapter One
The Ardrossan Estate

— 64

Chapter Two
Pool Pavilion

— 82

Chapter Three
Pool Cabana

— 120

Chapter Four
Ashwood Run

— 152

Concluding Thoughts
A Fireside Discussion between Author and Patron

— 274

Appendix

— 292

Bibliography

— 295

Project Credits

— 299

Acknowledgements

— 300

Book Credits

— 310

Foreword

by Peter Zimmerman

It is always rewarding when clients fully engage in the design process. I believe the design process is a thoughtful collaboration between the architect and client. Julieann and Keven Shanahan were engaged in the process and were essential to the development of the early concept of this multi-stage project. The Shanahans would give us feedback and we would react to it. It was very much the dialogue and the clients' vision that led us to the successful end result. The structures created different worlds for different seasons. From the basement renovation to the pool house, to the cabana, to a winter gathering place – all were creations of cozy family living spaces in very different environments. The one message we received clearly is that the Shanahans enjoy gathering with family and friends. Whether around a table enjoying an al fresco meal prepared in close proximity, gathering around a firepit on a cool summer evening, or a cozy winter night enjoying a warm fire and a spectacular view from a tree house perspective, the essence of all of this was having entertainment spaces appropriate and comfortable for each season that provide their own unique experiences and settings.

Peter Zimmerman Architects first started working with the Shanahans in 2015. They had just purchased the property on Ardrossan – a property that has a personal connection to my wife's side of the family. We were pleased to have the opportunity to be involved in a project that had such a beautiful, natural canvas. Prior to Keven and Julieann moving in, we did substantial reorganization and renovation of the first and second floors. We made the internal circulation work more efficiently creating a bedroom for their son and eliminating an exterior entrance to the second-floor in-law suite. As that project developed, we expanded down to a partially finished basement where we created family living with a kitchen and a bathroom where their children could have their own unique space. Exterior doors led to the outside for the ideal location of a pool and accompanying courtyard.

The next phase of design was the pool and a pool house pavilion. The criteria were to create a summer entertainment space with a focus on the pool where family and guests could cook, make pizza in the pizza oven, sit around a counter, dine at an outdoor dining table, or simply watch television and relax. A firepit and surround seating were created as an additional outside room and used as an active social space.

As we developed the pool house pavilion, there was the thought of creating an alternative space that had a different feeling to it – hence the inception of the cabana located at the opposite end of the pool and at a 90-degree angle to the pool pavilion. The space was totally open with a wonderful swinging day bed found by Julieann from a local vendor. The piece was the perfect selection as it became the focal point of the structure and spoke to the essence of the building which was very calming and gentle. The slight rocking of the daybed lent itself to meditation or a calm place in which to read or think—a passive, quiet space in contrast to the pool pavilion which centers more around poolside activities. The rear of the pavilion overlooks beautiful meadows that lead to an extending woodland area at the corner of the homeowner's property.

The final phase of this property plan is a structure called Ashwood Run. Its inspiration came from a pavilion at Blackberry Farm in Tennessee. This was a space in which I was fortunate enough to spend some time with good friends. We sat around a roaring fire; the food and drink were plentiful – it was the perfect winter entertainment space. Being familiar with that pavilion, I was able to understand what the Shanahans wanted and envisioned. The structure was primarily thought of as an open-air pavilion but with dining that surrounded an over-sized fireplace on two sides and the front. Directly behind the fireplace we located the services: a powder room on the first floor and a catering kitchen on the basement floor below. As we walked the proposed site, we found ourselves up against a woodland where a bank dropped down very steeply to a stream that meandered along the bottom of the hillside. There was a feeling of being surrounded by the tree canopies because the bank declined so precipitously. That feeling started the conversation about adding a loft that would

Peter Zimmerman is the Owner and a Principal of Peter Zimmerman Architects, Inc. Founded in 1982, the firm specializes in custom, residential architecture. Mr. Zimmerman provides design leadership in the firm while maintaining hands on involvement in all projects. In addition to the national recognition awarded to Peter Zimmerman Architects Inc. over the past 40 years, as part of his graduate studies, Mr. Zimmerman was awarded a grant from the prestigious Graham Foundation for the Continued Arts and served as editor of the *Harvard Architectural Review*. Specialties: Residential Architecture, Comprehensive Property Planning, Restoration, Renovations and Additions and Conservation Easements.

Mill Creek Terrace, Peter Zimmerman. Photo courtesy of Tom Crane.

create a treehouse experience that could be enjoyed by both children and adults alike. There is access through a ship's ladder to this wonderful, small space where one can enjoy nature and immediately relax. Through design development, it became clear that because of how the building was going to be used, it needed to be enclosed. We added folding aluminum doors, matching those we used at the pool house pavilion and cabana. When one visits these spaces and opens the doors, it truly feels like living outside. When used later into the season, the doors can be closed, and infrared heating elements allow the space to be used year-round.

Having the close familial connection to this property and working with Keven and Julieann made this a gratifying experience. Being part of what started as a renovation and then organically expanded into this extremely attractive, architecturally appropriate collection of pavilions that reflects three very different experiences, is something of which I am proud.

Prospector, Peter Zimmerman. Photography by Audrey Hall.
(Above and further above)

Setai, Peter Zimmerman. Photo courtesy of Tom Crane.

Foreword

Setai, Peter Zimmerman. Photo courtesy of Tom Crane.

Preface

by Julieann Shanahan

"In my view, building a house all by itself on a piece of land feels incomplete—you always need another structure or structures, as well as landscape experiences, to realize the promise of a home." ~ (Gil Schafer III)[1]

It never occurred to me that I would one day find myself a patron of architecture and a steward of a historic property. I began renovating as a hobby to tackle day-to-day functionality needs for a young family. But over time, I became more and more immersed in tinkering with home projects and fine-tuning renovations that led to an almost obsessive view of the big picture of how life would flow at our home. After nine years of serially renovating and updating our first home, we decided it was time to move on and put all our renovating lessons learned into the development of a comprehensive architectural design plan.

We embarked upon a new property search with earnestness and optimism. Two years later, we had zero prospects and a deluge of disappointment. We could not seem to find the ideal setting and location despite viewings of numerous properties. While eying one particular property with a potential tear down house on it, I started drawing a site map with a long switchback driveway leading to a main house up on a hill with smaller buildings behind it. When I presented the drawing to our realtor, she suggested that we would end up creating that setting ourselves and it would require a tremendous amount of work over a considerable amount of time. I completely abandoned the idea of finding or creating anything that looked like my original site map and threw it in the garbage bin.

Months later, we finally stumbled upon the house that would become our next home. I was captivated the minute I drove up the straight driveway lined with 29 Pear Blossom trees approaching the house. A large solitary field-stone house stood proudly without anything surrounding it other than a discreet two-car detached garage (fig. 0.1). There was a substantial woodland of trees entwined with overgrown underbrush about 120 feet from the back of the house. The house was situated on an interior flag lot with 360-degree views of undulating hills that were once used for fox hunting, as a dairy farm and corn fields. This specific piece of land was folded into the Ardrossan Estate in 1916 to expand an already majestic parcel. The house under consideration had been on the market for several years and needed a large-scale renovation to suit our family's daily life demands, but the skeletal floor plan was workable and welcoming.

We interviewed several architects and quickly settled on Peter Zimmerman. We liked Peter's approach to adhering to classical architecture principles while being able to deliver a wide variety of work and solutions. Soon after closing, the interior of the house was quickly demolished and

Fig. 0.1 | View of the home from the driveway through the tall grass, © Jeffrey Totaro, 2022

Julieann Shanahan is a financial professional with over 20 years' experience having worked in Vanguard's Investment Strategy Group, GE Capital, and Neuberger Berman. Her first job in finance was in Milan, Italy, working for an Italian family office where she developed a profound love of Italian culture and patrimony. Currently, she serves various philanthropic organizations including the Episcopal Academy Board of Trustees, and Children's Hospital of Philadelphia Foundation Board of Advisors. She has completed numerous renovation projects and remains an avid traveler to this day. This is her first book.

~

taken down to the studs. Although the house was nowhere near completion, we decided to start a pool project with a quiet unassuming pavilion. Perhaps it was a convoluted course to embark upon the outdoor living spaces before we completed indoor living, but we wanted to construct spaces that our children would use and remember most vividly about growing up in the house. Therefore, the formal living room and dining room were completed long after the pool and the first two pavilions.

Creating the pool and the first pavilion seemed like a natural extension of our home. We sought simple clean lined buildings that served multiple purposes. We wanted to be able to escape the sun, relax, cook, listen to music, watch sports and contain adequate storage (fig. 0.2). It was clear from the start that the pool itself was not just a form of recreation but a timeless architectural element to help bring people together.

We were very focused on what could yield a minimal amount of maintenance for an outbuilding in the northeastern United States. I did not want to install any additional plumbing lines that would require winterization and meticulous care. We wanted to be able to enclose the buildings easily to withstand the weather so collapsible accordion doors became the best solution. We already had a set of French doors exiting from a walk out basement to the pool area. It made sense to utilize part of the basement as an extension of the pool pavilion and create a completely separate living area with a half bathroom, swim changing area, bunk room, kitchenette, laundry room and storage closets. The basement area, the pool and the first pavilion comprised the original vision of an outdoor recreational space. But we were missing a focal point at the end of the pool.

We added a cabana at the end of the pool after the initial plans were drawn. This created a defined courtyard effect to feel privately ensconced within a larger setting of the rolling hills. The cabana resides at the base of the 20 x 40 foot pool and creates a focal point as the pool pavilion is hidden to the side flanking a large pre-existing retaining wall. The cabana houses a small swinging couch to provide the ultimate resting place on a sunny afternoon.

The first two buildings were small at about 250 and 500 square feet each. Our land is under Conservation Easement through the Brandywine Conservancy where we have a 1,500 square foot allotment for Accessory Structures – buildings that are incidental to the main house. We had about 750 square feet remaining and debated building a life-size playhouse (fig. 0.3). But we finally concluded that it would not have a long useful life given the ages of our children and relative expense of the project. We decided to reserve the allotment for a later project. In the meantime, we still worked on building out our house and family life which included frequent traveling.

Whenever I returned home from a trip, I yearned to replicate our experiences and feelings while on vacation – especially during family

Fig. 0.2 | Meadowcreek Arcanum Architecture. Inspiration for the pool pavilion.

dinners. After an amazing summer vacation in Stabbiano outside Lucca, Italy, with friends, it felt natural to attempt to build an Italian style loggia off of the house to complete a courtyard experience at the pool (fig. 0.4). But the Conservation Easement restricted any overhang to 14 feet. A loggia would have restricted light into a walk out basement which was a non-starter. So, we began with a real al fresco dining set up alongside the base of our pool. At first, I attempted to replicate a dining under the stars experience that we had in Punta Mita, Mexico (fig. 0.5). On more than one occasion, this left us running to seek shelter from the rain in the middle of dinner carrying our plates (fig. 0.6). Finally, I had a great idea for flag like tarps that I saw in Normandy, France to cover our dining area (fig. 0.7). Previously, I had custom string light poles made and envisioned hanging tarps to protect us from sun and light rain. But, in the end, the flag-like tarps didn't provide enough shelter. I was starting to give up on finding a reliable outdoor dining solution that would work for us.

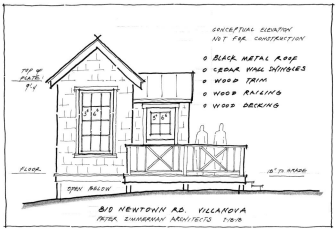

Fig. 0.3 | Peter Zimmerman Architects hand sketch of life-sized playhouse.

Then we took an unforeseen trip to Blackberry Farm in Tennessee. We were told to meet up at the Yallarhammer building to get ready for a fly-fishing lesson. Once I entered the building, I would not leave. I wandered around and stood in front of the fireplace, lollygagged eating a sandwich at the picnic table, located the bathroom, examined a kitchenette and discovered a large smoker at the back of building. I knew for sure that we could recreate this building, setting and feeling at our home (fig. 0.8). Like the evolution of pavilions in history, we moved inspiration-wise from an open-air setting to a tent to a hut-like building that was truly incorporated into the landscape to create the setting for enchanting family dinners.

I began the internal family campaign that we could use one last building on our property while everyone moaned in reluctant acquiescence. Our family was fatigued with construction and enduring the details of my next best great idea. To make it most palatable to everyone in the family, we combined the ideal family wants that remained for us into creating our version of the Blackberry Farm Yallarhammer. My husband wanted more garage space so we added a full basement with 9 ½ foot ceilings. All pool storage got moved into the basement and we freed up a garage bay. My daughters still wanted some form of a playhouse, so we added a small look out loft with a cantilevered balcony that serves as a naturalist's get away. My son wanted to see more elongated views of the land and the new building itself, so we added an outdoor firepit with panoramic views.

Within two months of the Tennessee trip, we started the architectural drawings of our largest pavilion with a 720 square foot footprint. I pitched my proposed location of a rolling hill that led to a swampy flat collection basin at our first architectural planning meeting. Peter Zimmerman meandered closer to where the wooded area began and declared that we should situate the building in front of the tree line. Right then, we all knew his proposed location was the right one.

Preface

Fig. 0.4 | Dinner in the loggia at Stabbiano, Italy. Photo by author.

Fig. 0.5 | Family style dinner on the beach at the St. Regis Punta Mita, Mexico. Photo by author.

Fig. 0.6 | Dinner party table setting opposite the Pool Pavilion. Photo by author.

Fig. 0.7 | Tarps providing shelter from the sun at a restaurant in Normandy, France. Photo by author.

Fig. 0.8 | Finding inspiration in the
Yallarhammer at Blackberry Farm. Photo by author.

Once I got everyone at home on board and re-enlisted the architect, designer and general contractor, I faced my biggest challenge yet – taming and pruning the woodland. The back woods were over-run with tangled brush and weeds. An added dilemma was that the underbrush was often tick infested due to deer traipsing through the woods. We met with the Conservancy and inventoried the indigenous, non-indigenous and landscape planted trees to see what we could remove with a clear conscience. We could barely walk into the area we were trying to revive.

The long-term goal was and still is to preserve the canopy tree line and make better use of the land. Unbeknownst to us, there was a small collection of decades old refuse hidden in the underbrush. First, we cleared out truckloads of rubbish including rubber tires, hub caps, hoses, rusted equipment, potting planters and beverage containers. After a series of crews visited with brush cutters and mowers, we were finally able to walk more freely and truly examine the trees. We cleared out the dead wood and a select group of non-indigenous trees including Paulownia trees, Cork trees and Norway Maples. We meticulously moved the new proposed building away from the drip line of a magnificent 60-year-old Beech tree. We decided to treat multiple Ash trees medicinally to stave off Emerald Ash Borer disease and trimmed dead wood off branches 70 feet from the ground to revive a stunning Tulip Poplar. The newly manicured timber range in age from nascent saplings to almost 140 years old and are in the sight line of the rear elevated look out loft of our latest pavilion. The land maintenance and rejuvenation will be an ongoing project for at least a decade if not longer, but we got things to a point where we could build and observe nature placidly – both for the observer and the creatures being observed. The land conservation and revival were critical to the construction of the last pavilion. We decided to name this final pavilion Ashwood Run as a tiny creek, Abrahams Run, runs behind the building and four Ash trees surround the building at various points.

In totality, we used our square footage allotment for three striking buildings all with unique purposes but tied together through architecture and design. The classical and vernacular architecture of the three buildings has given us great flexibility to design, nurture and live in the way that suits our family life. The outside buildings are a continuation of our home in terms of design elements and consistent materials. The delineation of separately defined spaces away from the house without the reminders of everyday life resulted in spaces that let us really unwind. In the end we created three folly houses meant to clear the mind, come together, and enjoy the scenery.

For a self-proclaimed city person, all these combined projects have presented a growth opportunity that I could not have taken on without a team of the highest caliber. I am eternally grateful to have had the great pleasure of collaborating with an architect, general contractor and designer who collectively have over 100 years of practical experience and have created a family life and salubrious way of living that we could not have experienced without them. The team has touched, designed and constructed not only the pavilions but every entry and exit point of our home – the front entry gate, the main entry door and the interior sequences that lead visitors to the new pavilions – to create a comprehensive design plan that is also respectful of the legacy of the land.

I hope you enjoy reading and viewing this book as much as I enjoyed working on it and the projects contained on the pages within. It is meant to share ideas and processes celebrating everyday family life and infusing fond memories.

Cheers, Julieann

Notes:
[1] Gil Schafer, *A Place to Call Home: Tradition, Style, and Memory in the New American House* (New York: Rizzoli, 2017): 48.

Introduction

Butterflies, Tents, and Wooden Huts: A Brief History of Pavilions

~

It is generally agreed that it is no mark of a foolish [person] to make sure of everything that would justify the care and expense of construction, and to ensure that the work itself is as lasting and salubrious as possible... Is an undertaking that leads to your own well-being, that favors a life of dignity and pleasure... not one of great benefit to yourself and your family?... I am of the opinion, therefore, that there is nothing, aside from virtue to which a [person] should devote more care, more effort and attention, than to the acquisition of a good home to shelter [themself] and [their] family (Leon Battista Alberti).[1]

Fig. 0.9 | Loggia and Odeon Cornaro, Padua, Italy. Giovanni Maria Falconetto, 1524–30. Scala Archives, 0047297.

The great Renaissance humanist and architect, Leon Battista Alberti, argued in his treatise *On the Art of Building* that the highest good was that of the public realm and that the primary goal of every individual was to be a model citizen. The architect was therefore a kind of gifted civic activist, conditioned by *virtù* (virtue) to achieve excellence in building with the aim of fulfilling the highest needs of mankind. Yet the architect also needed enlightened patrons to understand the great importance of a healthy and dignified built environment, especially at the level of domestic building. His simple plea for architectural patronage resonated profoundly with princes, nobles, popes, and kings, but it also found a captured audience in like-minded humanists and enlightened individuals throughout Italy.

Among the many Renaissance patrons who deliberately responded to Alberti's claim was the Italian humanist, Alvise Cornaro, a nobleman from Padova who at the age of eighty-three wrote *A Sober Life* (1558), a eulogy of moderation and leisure that proclaimed the joys of health and longevity.[2] A leading figure in the city's humanist circle, he dedicated his life to balancing the activities of landowner with interests in literature and architecture. His house in Padova contained the first *all'antica* (in the ancient manner) buildings in the Veneto, a Loggia (1524) and Odeon (1530) designed by Giovanni Maria Falconetto, a painter and architect from Verona who had previously studied in Rome (fig. 0.9).[3] The two structures were essentially free-standing pavilions placed perpendicular to one another in the garden behind the house, with the Loggia at the far end opposite the rear façade and the Odeon in between the two facing the garden's center. The Loggia, open to the garden with an arcaded façade, was used for outdoor entertaining and dining whereas the Odeon, an enclosed structure with an octagonal room at its center with magnificent frescos by Giovanni da Udine, was used for chamber music performances and other intellectual activities. (fig. 0.10) The Loggia was given a second story when the Odeon was constructed, and the two pavilions were connected by an arched wall creating a re-entrant

corner that transformed the garden into an outdoor room, or theater if you will. It was here, in the garden and pavilions, that Cornaro housed his humanist academy, and where Sebastiano Serlio, Andrea Palladio, and other Renaissance architects and artists were exposed to modern ideas on classical music, art, literature, and well-being *(benessere)*.

Like Alberti, Cornaro was deeply concerned with the art of building, producing a *Treatise on Architecture* (c. 1550-1553) that aimed at addressing the private residences of average citizens rather than aristocrats.[4] Central to his treatise was the belief that architecture's main purpose was to afford infinite pleasure, comfort, and satisfaction, arguing that a building "honestly beautiful but perfectly comfortable" was more desirable than one which was "supremely beautiful but uncomfortable."[5]

Cornaro's example is but one of many Italian Renaissance projects that clearly demonstrates how a close relationship between patron and architect can produce an exceptional and unexpected solution for a healthy and meaningful domestic garden setting. What makes it so unusual, however, is that it was achieved at an incredibly modest scale by a well-intentioned humanist visionary. And even though Cornaro came from an elite patrician family from Venice that included several Doges, Cardinals, Bishops and other high officials, the simple transformation of his house and garden into a leading intellectual center was in fact a very wise endeavor that made an enormous difference in the life of the city. In that sense, Cornaro's example continues to resonate today among thoughtful patrons of architecture, and his two little garden structures for his house in Padova, set an exacting standard for what pavilion living can be.

Of course, pavilions were not invented during the Italian Renaissance. In fact, they are among the oldest and most enjoyed building types in existence, evolving from tent-like structures into free-standing or semi-detached open buildings used largely as a place for entertainment and recreation. Originally derived from the Latin *papilion*,

Victor Deupi is a Senior Lecturer at the University of Miami School of Architecture. His research focuses on the early modern Spanish and Ibero-American world, mid-20th-century Cuba, and contemporary architecture. His books include *Architectural Temperance* (2015), *Transformations in Classical Architecture* (2018), *Emilio Sanchez in New York and Latin America* (2020), *Cuban Modernism*, with Jean-Francois Lejeune (2021), *Emilio Sanchez Revisited*, with LnS Gallery (2021), and *Stables* and *Wineries of the World*, both with Oscar Riera Ojeda (2021). *Pavilion Living* is his fifth book with Oscar Riera Ojeda Publishers.

referring to a butterfly or moth, the term most likely came about from army slang regarding the entrance of a military tent, where the end coverings were turned over and fastened up at the sides to allow access inside, and in doing so created a shape resembling the wings of a fluttering insect (fig. 0.11).[6] They were also much more ornamental, made of finer materials of varied colors than an ordinary tent *(tentorium)*, hence the more expressive terminology. Because of their simple mobility, tents were an essential form of portable shelter for nomadic, military, and court ceremonial purposes and were described by ancient writers and confirmed in early pictorial records. The same constructional principles continued well into medieval Europe and further afield in the Middle East, Central Asia, Africa, and pre-Columbian America. In medieval French, *pavillon* replaced the Latin term which was then simply anglicized to create the modern English equivalent. Throughout Europe though, the term pavilion was consistently associated with ornamental buildings of light construction and its use in other Romance languages such as Spanish *(pabellón)*, or Italian *(padiglione)*, basically meant the same thing. In a related sense, there are two Latin words for tent, tentorium which as already mentioned refers to a common tensile structure stretched upon taut cords, and *tabernaculum*, meaning formed with planks and covered with skins or woven canvas, both being interchangeable.[7] Coincidentally, in Jewish history, the Feast of Tabernacles is a festival commemorating the Israelites' encampments during their sojourn in the wilderness. We also find that the Tabernacle refers to the curtained tent containing the Ark of the Covenant and other sacred relics which served as a portable sanctuary until the Israelites settled in Jerusalem and constructed the Temple Mount (fig. 0.12). Further east in Turkish and Persian cultures the word kiosk (from *kiushk* and *kuskh* respectively) was used instead of pavilion to refer to ornamental garden structures or palace porticos. In the Far East, the Chinese words *dian* and *tang* (hall or pavilion) and *t'ing* (kiosk) were largely interchangeable, whereas in Southeast Asia, the pavilion referred to

Fig. 0.10 | Odeon Cornaro, Padua, Italy, Giovanni Maria Falconetto, fresco by Giovanni da Udine (Giovanni Ricamatore), 1524 – 1526, Fondazione Federico Zeri - Università di Bologna, Photo Archive.

Fig. 0.11 | Model of a Roman tent, called *papilio* (butterfly), ca.122-128 CE, Tullie House Museum and Art Gallery, Carlisle, Cumbria, England, photo by Manuel Cohen, Scala Archives, MC16656C

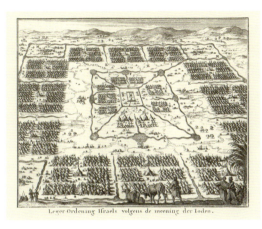

Fig. 0.12 | The Tabernacle Surrounded by the Camps of the Twelve Tribes of Israel, etching, Jan Luyken, Rijksmuseum, Amsterdam, 1683, acc. no. RP-P-1896-A-19368-331

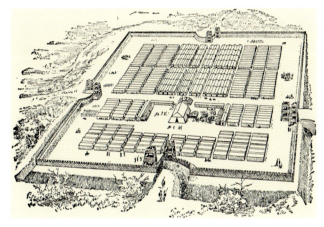

0.13 | Roman Camp, from Wilbur F. Gordy, *American Beginnings in Europe* (New York: Charles Scribner's Sons, 1912), © 2004–2022 Florida Center for Instructional Technology, University of South Florida

a wide variety of structures including a *gopura* (entry pavilion or porch), *mandapa* (a Buddhist reliquary), and *sala* (kiosk), completing the ancient and global etymology of the term. Clearly, the pavilion is a highly valued architectural structure that crosses global cultural traditions in a way that few building types - other than the house - have ever achieved with such simplicity and clarity of purpose. And while pavilions could be found in a variety of settings throughout the world, they particularly flourished in the domestic realm.

Pavilions first emerged in the ancient world for their mobility and to facilitate the construction of temporary military encampments. The Greek historian Polybius (ca. 200-117 BCE) was the earliest writer to discuss Roman marching camps - as opposed to permanent garrison towns - in Book VI of *The Histories*, describing them as having been constructed of earthen ramparts with timber stockades and filled with tents instead of purpose-built barracks (fig. 0.13).[8] Having witnessed

first-hand several of these camps, his lengthy account, however, makes no mention of the construction of tents or their entryways. A century later, the Roman architect and writer Vitruvius, following many Greek predecessors, outlined his own vision of the origins of building in his treatise *De architectura* (*On Architecture*, ca. 25 BCE), describing the timber-framed hut as the model and source for subsequent buildings, especially houses.[9] Vitruvius' account largely follows that of the Roman philosopher Lucretius (ca. 99-55 BCE), whose book *De rerum natura* (On the Nature of Things) provided the first secular account of human culture, suggesting that authority for current practices could be found in the natural origins of mankind. To be sure, ancient speculations on the origins of building often concluded that pavilions and other temporary structures evolved from either the primary forms of stick-and-cloth tent combinations or through deliberate carpenter's work, or a combination of both. Early depictions of Roman encampments can be seen in several relief panels from the Column of Trajan in Rome (113 CE) where

Fig. 0.14 | Roman Camp, reproduced from a bas-relief from the Column of Trajan (53-117 CE), Museo della Civilta Romana, Scala Archives, WH37981.

marching soldiers and purification rituals could be seen with open tents behind them (fig. 0.14).[10] Much later, sometime in the early 4th century, the Roman writer Aelius Lampridius, author of four biographies in the *Historia Augusta*, used the term *papilionibus* to describe the open military tents where the emperor Severus Alexander (reg. 222-35 CE) dined with his soldiers eating ordinary food to their great pleasure.[11] In the following century on the morning of October 28, 312 CE, Constantine defeated Maxentius at the Battle of the Milvian Bridge to become the undisputed Emperor of Rome. On the evening before battle, he had a vision of a cross in the sky with the command "In this sign you will conquer," an image that was famously captured in the mid-fifteenth century by Piero della Francesca at the Basilica of San Francesco in Arezzo, Italy (fig. 0.15).[12] Whatever the circumstances, it is clear that the early evolution of the pavilion as an architectural type came from the ornamental tent, and its use in ancient Rome became widespread, especially in private residences where house and garden could be mediated by any number of detached or semi-detached open structures that were used for entertainment and leisure.

Among the best examples of ancient Roman pavilions are those found at Nero's Domus Aurea on the Esquiline hillside in Rome, and Hadrian's Villa just outside of Tivoli. Nero's hillside villa, built shortly after the Great Fire of 64 CE, contained a great circular dining pavilion on the west-facing wing with a large oculus and adjacent spill-out rooms that could rotate day and night in sync with the heavens. An outdoor terrace extended from the dining pavilion overlooking the Roman Forum and eventually the Colosseum which was built in 80 CE. Hadrian's Villa (c. 125-34 CE) was a large complex composed of multiple buildings and several loosely joined pavilions surrounding atrium courts and peristyle gardens. Constructed as a summer retreat where the emperor and his entourage could relax from everyday life, the pavilions on the property contained libraries (both Greek and Roman), a circular island

Fig. 15 | Legend of the True Cross: Constantine's Dream, Church of San Francesco, Arezzo, Italy, Piero della Francesca, c. 1452, Scala Archives, 0123320.

guest house, and an isolated square tower surmounted by a circular domed structure. Hadrian's Villa embodied the idea of leisure at a monumental scale and therefore became one of the most influential monuments in the history of architecture.

Less flamboyant villas could be found throughout the Roman empire with suburban villas serving as leisure retreats for city dwellers, and rustic villas functioning as working farms, and in the former case, pavilions fulfilled the much more domestic purpose of facilitating rest and relaxation. Intellectual and physical activity (*otium* in Latin) - the inverse of what typically occurred in the city in terms of business *(negotium)* - was the main purpose of leisure. The wealthy landowner, Pliny the Younger for instance, described in his letters his sumptuous seaside villa in Laurentum, just outside of Rome, and the joy he derived from staying there.[13] The villa had elegantly decorated bedrooms, bathing suites, and sumptuous gardens, with a fine dining room with foldable doors and windows around three sides that opened directly to the sea allowing the spray from the breakers to lightly wash the interiors, if not the visitors. Elsewhere in the garden, a sunroom *(heliocaminus)* faced a terrace on one side, the sea on the other, and the sun on three sides. Similar villas with leisure pavilions could be found in the Tuscan hills, on the slopes of Vesuvius just outside of Pompeii and Herculaneum, on the Isle of Capri, in Sicily, and throughout the empire from Egypt to Britain.

In ancient Chinese architecture, a one or two-story hall structure is known as a *dian* or *tang*. It is distinguished from the *t'ing*, translated as a pavilion-style pagoda, which is more like a kiosk. Pavilions were commonly employed in Buddhist monastic complexes such as the Dule Monastery in the Hebei Province, from 741-984 CE, which contains a one-story gateway pavilion (fig. 0.16), and a three-story, timber-framed structure, the Guanyin Hall, housing a colossal clay

Fig. 0.16 | Shan Gate, Dule Temple, Tianjin China, 984 CE, licensed under the Creative Commons Attribution-Share Alike 4.0 International

statue of the *bodhisattva*.[14] Pavilions could also be found in silk paintings or on wall murals such as those found in the Mogao caves in the Gansu Province from approximately 618-907 CE.[15] The Chinese kiosk was typically a garden structure consisting of a covered roof supported by decorative pillars.[16] Having a dual function of both being an object in the garden and a protected place from which to observe the landscape, the kiosk came in a great variety of shapes and could be found beside pools, on hills, or in groves of trees. These structures reinforced the main purpose of the Chinese garden as a place to retreat from the everyday world and nourish the heart.

In the Islamic world, the kiosk flourished as an ornamental garden pavilion that could range from a light wooden structure to a monumental masonry form. Throughout the Mediterranean, Islamic kiosks could be found in gardens in the Near East, North Africa, Sicily,

Fig. 0.17 | Patio de la Acequia, Generalife, Andalusia, Granada, early 14th century, licensed under the Creative Commons Attribution-Share Alike 4.0 International

Fig. 0.18 | Baghdad Kiosk, Topkapı Palace, Istanbul, Turkey, 1639, licensed under the Creative Commons Attribution-Share Alike 3.0 Unported

and Spain. The Nasrid dynasty (1230-1492), the last Arab court in Spain, developed a form of garden pavilion, a glorified belvedere, set within the fortified palace of the Alhambra overlooking Granada that allowed water, light, and shade to be distributed in a series of room and courtyard sequences providing great pleasure to visitors and residents alike.[17] Outside the Alhambra walls and located nearby to the east was the Generalife, the summer palace of the Nasrid rulers with courtyards, gardens, fountains, open pavilions on the north and south ends of the main patio, and a *mirador* (meaning viewing) tower for overlooking the gardens and landscape beyond (fig. 0.17).

Among the most splendid residential examples are those at the Ottoman court at Istanbul, where the Sultan, Mehmed II (reg 1444–81), erected several kiosks in the gardens of the Topkapı Palace at the southernmost peninsula of the ancient city high above the Bosphorus Strait.[18] The Sultan had three pavilions constructed in the outer palace gardens and several others far below overlooking the shore for his viewing pleasure. Of those that have survived, the Baghdad Kiosk of 1639 is an impressive example of an Ottoman room, with highly ornate interiors, sumptuous lounging areas, and a tiled central dome (figs. 0.18-19). Perhaps the greatest concentration of Islamic kiosks can be found in the gardens of the royal palace at Isfahan, Iran, under the Safavid (reg 1501–1732) dynasty.[19] For the Persians, the garden represented an image of Paradise, with water a fundamental source of life in the parched Iranian desert. Trees, flowers, birds, and animals gave further vitality to the garden, inspiring representations in carpets, tapestries, and other decorative patterns. The pavilion was typically set within the garden scattered among trees or framing a pool in a much more central location. The imperial palace at Isfahan contained several of these garden pavilions, mostly on a grand scale with both indoor and outdoor spaces, lofty porches, elaborate geometric tile patterns, and marble fountains (fig. 0.20). Such ornamental garden structures could be used for receiving visiting dignitaries, guests of the royal family, courtiers, and of course, women of the harem.

Fig. 0.19 | Baghdad Kiosk, Topkapı Palace, Istanbul, Turkey, interior, 1639, photo by Maksym Kozlenko, licensed under the Creative Commons Attribution-Share Alike 4.0 International

The Ottoman and Persian examples were contemporary with Leon Battista Alberti's writings on architecture, just as Italian Renaissance architects began reviving ancient building practices for contemporary purposes, often in the form of conjectural reconstructions. For instance, the highly influential *Hypnerotomachia Poliphili* (1499), a dream-like illustrated treatise on art presumably by a Venetian Dominican friar named Francesco Colonna, described in detail the garden's reliance on fountains, inscriptions, statues, and pavilions (0.21).[20] At some point in the mid-sixteenth century, Sebastiano Serlio published his eighth book on architecture titled *Castramentation of the Romans* following Polybius's description.[21] In the preface he mentioned the great pleasure he took from the design and measurements of the "pavilions, wooden huts, and tents" that

Fig. 0.20 | Pavilion of Chehel Sotoun, Isfahan, Iran, 1647, photo by Arad Mojtahedi, licensed under the Creative Commons Attribution-Share Alike 4.0 International.

the ancient author had described previously, and in his plan reconstructions of the temporary camps, he labeled the individual officer's sleeping quarters as *tenda* (tent) and *padiglione* (pavilion) interchangeably without regard to their shape being round or rectangular. Wooden watchtowers and open sheds, on the other hand, were presented as huts in the form of archetypal structures.

Around the same time, the Venetian architect Andrea Palladio developed a new type of villa, merging ancient suburban and rustic villas into modern country estates for gentleman farmers.[22] Modest in scale and ornamentation, the villas contained open loggias that were perfect places to eat outdoors, converse with friends, or listen to music during the summer months. They were also largely surrounded by walled enclosures that included pavilions *(barchesse)* containing subsidiary functions such as barns, dovecotes, sheds, stables, wineries, and other farm uses that established a clear social presence in the countryside. Though Palladio did not include any free-standing or semi-detached pavilions like those of Alvise Cornaro in Padova, his villas and adjacent farm structures were instrumental in setting a new standard for living well in the countryside, noting in his *Four Books on Architecture* (1572) that:

[h]ouses in cities really are splendid and convenient for the gentleman, since he has to live in them throughout the period that he needs for the administration of the community and running his own affairs. But he will perhaps find the buildings on his estate no less useful and comforting, where he will pass the rest of the time watching over and improving his property and increasing his wealth through his skill in farming, and where, by means of the exercise that one usually takes on the country estate on foot or on horseback, his body will more readily maintain its healthiness and strength, and where, finally, someone whose spirit is tired by the aggravations of the city will be revitalized, soothed, and will be able to attend in tranquility to the study of literature and quiet contemplation; similarly this was why the sensible men of the ancient world made a habit of withdrawing frequently to such places where, visited by brilliant friends and relatives, they could easily pursue the good life to be enjoyed there since they had lodgings, gardens, fountains, and similar soothing locales. And above all their own virtù.[23]

Further south in Rome, the detached pavilion became a particularly popular garden structure in Renaissance landscape villas, especially in the late-sixteenth century with the rise of *villegiatura* (the conscious departure from cities during the summer to avoid

Introduction

Fig. 0.21 | Satyr with Sleeping Nymph, woodcut illustration from the *Hypnerotomachia Poliphili*, Francesco Colonna, published by Aldo Manuzio, Venice, 1499, Metropolitan Museum of Art, acc. no. 23.73.1

the heat and engage in healthy mental and physical activity by the sea or in the countryside) among the papacy, church officials, and other ruling magnates.[24] Among the best examples are the Casino of Pope Pius IV (1558–61) in the Vatican gardens by Pirro Ligorio, and the *palazzine* of the Villa Lante (1566) in Bagnaia presumably by Giacomo Barozzi da Vignola. The Casino, or small house, of Pius IV, was an afternoon retreat for the Pope easily accessible from the papal palace by foot, consisting of several small buildings arranged around a semi-enclosed courtyard (fig. 0.22-23). Entry gates, a dining pavilion in the form of an ancient tomb, and a small pleasure house formed the charming complex that was perched on a hill with views across the landscape. The Villa Lante was the garden estate of Cardinal Gianfrancesco Gambara, Bishop of Viterbo, whose property contained twin *palazzine* (small palaces or casinos), a formal garden and a hunting park, sloping uphill from the medieval town of Bagnaia (0.24). The identical cubic pavilions flanked a zig-zag ramp both having an open loggia overlooking the formal square garden below, and private suites on the upper floor, with a belvedere pavilion as a lantern on the pyramidal roof. The simple forms recall the rural structures of the Italian countryside whereas the exterior stone facing, classical detailing, and frescoed interiors resemble miniature urban palaces (fig. 0.25). All around Rome, from Caprarola to the north, Tivoli to the east, and Frascati to the south, those who could afford to build sumptuous private villas did so with great energy and zeal making the outdoor pavilion a recurring theme of the Roman countryside well into the eighteenth century, setting the standard for outdoor living and entertainment away from city life during the oppressive Mediterranean summers.

In Renaissance France, a particular form of pavilion emerged as an element of architectural composition, typically in the form of a central or terminal section of a palace façade that projected forward as a pavilion-like bay culminating in a pedimented, domed, or hipped roof condition. This kind of pavilion, even if it overlooked a garden, was not a free-standing leisure building per se, and however fascinating the motif was in French Renaissance architecture, it contributed little to the tradition of garden pavilions. French landscaped gardens, however, especially the hunting lodges of the French kings which were turned into villas with formal gardens, featured prominent ornamental pavilions.[25] Several examples could be found at Versailles in the gardens of the Petit Trianon, built for Louis XV's chief mistress, Madame de Pompadour, that included the French Pavilion (1750) and the Cool Pavilion (1753), both by Anges-Jacques Gabriel, and the Belvedere Pavilion (1778-79) by Richard Mique. The French Pavilion was located at the center

Fig. 0.22 | Casino di Pio IV, Vatican Gardens, Italy, Pirro Ligorio, 1559-62, photo by author.

Fig. 0.23 | Casino of Pio IV, Vatican Gardens, Italy, Pirro Ligorio, 1559-62, photo by author.

Fig. 0.24 | Casino at the Villa Lante, Bagnaia, Italy, Giacomo Barozzi (Vignola), 1560s, photo by author.

Introduction

of the formal garden in the form of a large circular room flanked by four smaller rooms that extended diagonally and served as a boudoir, wardrobe, kitchen, and warming room (figs. 0.26-27). Clad in stone with urns crowning the cornice and large windows opening onto the garden, the French Pavilion was decorated inside with mirrors, gilded woodwork, and elegant tile paving, all in a discreet Rococo vocabulary. Nearby and directly on axis with the French Pavilion was the Cool Pavilion which served as a summer dining room where one could enjoy the cool fresh air and taste the produce grown in the nearby garden. The pavilion consisted of a single room and was conceived as a vegetal folly, entirely covered with a delicate wood lattice painted green. Finally, the Belvedere (meaning beautiful view), or Music Pavilion built for Queen Marie Antoinette, was set in a picturesque landscape, and consisted of a single-room octagonal structure capped by a shallow dome, the whole of which was perched on an artificial mound overlooking a reflecting pond and man-made grotto (fig. 0.28). Similar in character to the French Pavilion, the Belvedere contains several relief panels on the exterior above the doors and in the pediments that reference the pleasures of hunting, gardening, and the passage of time across the four seasons. Finally, at the Chateau de Louveciennes just outside of Paris, Claude-Nicolas Ledoux designed a Music Pavilion (1770–71) for Louis XV's last mistress, Madame Du Barry, with a suite of *en filade* reception rooms where the two could meet in privacy while overlooking the valley of the Seine (fig. 0.29). The discreet neoclassical architecture of the pavilion with elegant interiors was the perfect setting for small social gatherings, intimate dinners, or private affairs.

It should be noted that in addition to these Greco-Roman inspired examples, one could also find many non-classical pavilions throughout France, including the Hameau (1782-85), or farmer's hamlet by Richard Mique, that Marie Antoinette had constructed in the Trianon's picturesque garden, the last of the royal commissions at Versailles before the Revolution. Here you could find any number

Fig. 0.25 | Casino at the Villa Lante, Bagnaia, Italy, Giacomo Barozzi (Vignola), 1560s, photo by Max Hutzel, © Getty Research Institute Digital Collections, acc. no. 86.P.8

Fig. 0.26 | French Pavilion, Petit Trianon, Versailles, France, Anges-Jacques Gabriel, 1750, photo by Gilles Messian, licensed under the Creative Commons Attribution 2.0 Generic

of bucolic farm structures including a dairy, mill, dovecote, barn, or tower, all parading as cleverly designed leisure pavilions around an artificial lake. Similarly, Chinese-inspired follies in the form of decorative tents, pagodas, swings, and philosopher's pavilions could also complement any number of chateau gardens. Finally Dutch windmills, Turkish mosques, Tartar tents from central Asia, stone-and-thatch hermitages, miniature pyramids, and Gothic ruins could also be found littered throughout the countryside as pleasure pavilions of the most exotic sort.

The English crown was not as ambitious as the French, at least not at first, with limited resources resulting in the continued use of rural castles instead of newly built palaces. In Elizabethan England, however, garden structures emerged as banqueting halls for dessert courses after a main feast, or they took the form of belvedere roof pavilions as can be found at Longleat in Wiltshire, providing sheltered outdoor entertaining and banqueting spaces with endless views over the natural landscape.[26] In the early seventeenth century, Inigo Jones designed a Palladio-inspired cubic house in Greenwich for Anne of Denmark, queen to James I, marking the beginning of a new trend in England in which Palladio's influence would become particularly robust among country gentlemen. This coupled with the advent of the picturesque landscape garden gave pavilions a new importance in the eighteenth century. Follies, reconstructed buildings from antiquity, gazebos, miniature castles, artificial ruins, and other fantasy concoctions all contributed to making pavilions the eye-catching garden structures of the English country house.

At Castle Howard in North Yorkshire, the square Temple of the Four Winds (1724-26) with four Ionic porticoes by Sir John Vanbrugh, and the double-cylinder peripteral Mausoleum (1728-29) by Nicholas Hawksmoor, are among the most monumental free-standing pavilions in England, merging ancient Roman and Palladian precedents culminating in domed lanterns that convey a rural magnificence at an unprecedented scale. More modest than the Castle Howard examples is William Chambers' Casino at Marino (1759) in Dublin for James Caulfeild, the 1st Earl of Charlemont and a regular on the Roman Grand Tour. The deceptively small structure is often credited as the finest garden pavilion of its kind in Europe, designed as a Greek cross in plan set on a stepped platform and surrounded by Doric pediments, trabeated aediculas, and re-entrant corner porches. Even more discreet are the garden pavilions at Stourhead in Wiltshire, designed by the amateur architect, Henry Hoare II, that are strategically situated around a lake and are discovered by serendipity as one wanders through

Introduction

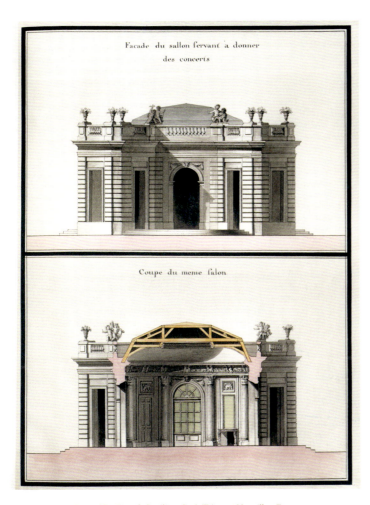

Fig. 0.27 | French Pavilion, Petit Trianon, Versailles, France, Anges-Jacques Gabriel, 1750, façade and section drawn by Richard Mique, from Recueil des plans du Petit Trianon, Folio 10, Biblioteca Estense, Modena, Italy, A. Dagli Orti/Scala, Florence, DG00435.

Fig. 0.28 | Le Rocher et le Belvédère à Versailles (The Rock and Belvedere at Versailles), oil on canvas, Claude-Louis Châtelet, 1785, © Château de Versailles, Dist. RMN.

Fig. 0.29 | Pavillon de Musique, Château de Louveciennes, France, Claude Nicolas Ledoux, 1770–71, photo by Jean-Marie Hullot, licensed under the Creative Commons Attribution–Share Alike 4.0 International.

Fig. 0.30 | Stourhead Gardens, Wiltshire, England, Henry Hoare II, 1741-80, photo by author.

the fascinating romantic landscape garden (fig. 0.30). The pavilions include a small Pantheon or Temple of Hercules (1754-56), a round Temple to Apollo based on a ruin from Baalbek (1765), and other bucolic structures such as a rustic cottage and a stone bridge. Finally at Stowe in Buckinghamshire, one finds not only a stately Palladian mansion, but also an extraordinary landscape by Lancelot "Capability" Brown, with a series of garden pavilions that include two open-porched Doric lake pavilions facing one another by John Vanbrugh (1719), two small square funerary structures with pyramidal tops called the Boycott Pavilions (1728-29 and named after a long lost local village) by James Gibbs, a circular Temple of Ancient Virtue by William Kent (1737, fig. 0.31), and a covered Palladian Bridge (1744, fig. 0.32), quite possibly by Gibbs, in imitation of a similar one designed by the 9th Earl of Pembroke (the "Architect Earl") and Roger Morris at the Wilton House in Wiltshire (1737). Capability Brown's landscape design at Stowe, having worked there as the Head Gardener from 1741-51, is not only one of his finest artistic experiments but also the first of his many transformations of the English countryside. Brown became so successful at renovating gardens in the late eighteenth century that his near contemporary and friend, the poet Richard Owen Cambridge, famously remarked that he hoped to die before Capability Brown so that he could see Heaven before it was improved.[27]

Throughout the early modern period in Europe, pleasure pavilions could be found in any number of Royal palaces, country estates, and public parks. In Spain for instance, the *Reales Sitios* (Royal Palaces) of San Ildefonso La Granja (1720-58) near Segovia, and Aranjuez (started in the 16th century with major additions from 1715-77) south of Madrid, contained 18th-century gardens where the new Bourbon monarchy in Spain could enjoy their leisure time in imitation of Versailles and other French country

Fig. 0.31 | Temple of Ancient Virtue, Stowe House and Gardens, Buckinghamshire, England, William Kent, 1737, photo by author.

houses.[28] As the grandson of Louis XIV, Philip V - the first Bourbon monarch in Spain - brought with him French designers and ideas to construct the new royal palace and gardens of La Granja alongside several Spanish counterparts. The gardens by René Carlier with sculptures by René Frémin, rival in layout if not in the grandeur of its waterworks, the magnificence of Versailles, with fountains, baths, a monumental cascade, and several pavilions

Fig. 0.32 | Palladian Bridge, Stowe House and Gardens, Buckinghamshire, England, James Gibbs, 1738, photo by author.

(fig. 0.33). The Royal Palace at Aranjuez had a series of enclosed formal gardens as early as the sixteenth century. Philip V commissioned the creation of the new Prince's Garden (1729) in the form of an English picturesque landscape with several recreational structures by Juan de Villanueva, including a small circular Ionic temple and a wooden Chinese pavilion facing one another across a small pond (fig. 0.34).

Philip V's son, Charles (Carlo di Borbone in Italian as his mother was Elizabeth Farnese), built the colossal Royal Palace at Caserta (1752-72) in the hills north of Naples where he was made King of the Imperial possessions from 1734-59, before he returned to Spain as Carlos III. Here, a seemingly endless two-mile cascade and canal with fountains and statuary descended from a distant mountain on axis with the main palace, which was designed by the Italian architect Luigi Vanvitelli, who coincidentally supervised the construction of the gardens as well. An English picturesque pleasure garden with palm trees and other exotic species (1785), laid out by Vanvitelli's son, Carlo, and the English landscape designer John Andrew Graefer, extended from the top of the cascade in a parallel direction with several follies, a lake and canal, artificial ruins, and pavilions, including a circular tempietto and a gothic chapel.[29] The informal garden was also married to the typical Italian "botanical garden" and thus it contained several greenhouses, a nursery, exotic flora, and an extensive herbarium, culminating in an extraordinary place to contemplate nature by experiencing it.

It goes without saying that the rise of pleasure pavilions, follies, and other garden buildings coincided with the representation of these structures by artists throughout Europe, usually in graphite sketches, engravings, watercolors, and oil paintings as a kind of post-occupancy evaluation of their fascination and use by their owners and guests. Just as the architecture of the new pavilions imitated ancient

Fig. 0.33 | Pavilion (or Marble Summer House) and Fountain of the Three Graces, Royal Place of San Ildefonso "La Granja," Segovia, Spain, René Carlier and René Frémin, 1720s, photo by Ignacio Revuelta, licensed under the Creative Commons Attribution–Share Alike 4.0 International.

forms, so too did their modern representations, taking inspiration from surviving wall paintings from Pompeii and Herculaneum, or *grotteschi* (grotto-like decorations of naturalistic elements) from Nero's Domus Aurea and other archaeological sites. Often depicted with a fantasy element, in ruins, or as a banquet scene set in a picturesque landscape, these capricious *(capriccio)* representations were much more than simply views *(vedute)* of existing buildings, they were pictorial souvenirs of great artistic interpretation and imagination. Additionally, pavilions would often be decorated inside with works of art at a variety of scales, from large murals to miniature scenes painted on furniture or in decorative arts objects like ceramics and tiles, and of course commissioned portraits would complete the representational schema.

In the Modern Era, pavilions became important elements of exhibition architecture across the globe.[30] Beginning with the 1851 Great Exhibition in London, the first large-scale industrial and cultural exhibition in which several nations from around the world exhibited their machinery, fine arts, and other manufactured products to promote economic and cultural trade, architecture was evident inside and out. The main exhibition hall, the Crystal Palace – as it was dubbed in the British satirical journal *Punch* – was a large, prefabricated glass and iron structure designed by the horticulturalist and engineer, Joseph Paxton, to showcase the latest trends in design and manufacturing. Interestingly, among the novel designs on display, a vernacular hut from Trinidad was exhibited as an example of the inherent simplicity and common-sense of indigenous building practices, a nod to what architecture should strive for in the future. The Crystal Palace and the primitive hut could be seen in tandem sharing similar qualities and design approaches that were largely devoid of historical styles or precedent.

Efforts to achieve such a straightforward architecture, expressed purely through materials and methods of construction without any reference

Introduction

to architectural styles, met with mixed results, especially in the arena of international exhibitions. The *Exposition Universelle* in Paris in 1867, for instance, featured many international pavilions representing the architectural culture of each nation in its most immersive form.[31] Situated on the city's great parade ground, the *Champ de Mars* (Field of Mars), the main exhibition hall consisted of a great covered amphitheater-like building made of iron surrounded by nearly 100 smaller buildings that included European, Asian, and Latin American pavilions. Several decades later in 1889, the *Exposition Universelle* in Paris that celebrated the centenary of the French Revolution featured the Eiffel Tower and the *Galerie des Machines*, both novel technological advancements in structural design. Yet despite these innovative structures a great deal of the exhibition contained a series of national and colonial pavilions flanking the River Seine and the Esplanade des Invalides with their respective historical attributes.

Fig. 0.34 | Ionic Temple and Chinese Pavilion, Jardín del Príncipe, Aranjuez, Spain, ca. 1750, photo by Ángel Serrano Sánchez de León, licensed under the Creative Commons Attribution-Share Alike 3.0 Unported.

The World's Columbian Exposition of 1893 in Chicago similarly included novel architecture such as Louis Sullivan's Transportation Building, and a Great Ferris Wheel, though overall the exhibition was dubbed the "White City" for its conspicuous association with monochromatic Greco-Roman inspired classical buildings.

The twentieth century truly introduced modern architecture to exhibition pavilions beginning with the Venice Biennale which took the lead in creating a multidisciplinary event that embraced several artistic disciplines, including music, cinema, theater, and dance.[32] With significant international participation, a series of dedicated pavilions were created within the public gardens (Giardini di Castello) where the biennial was held, creating the first global museum of modern architecture. The 1925 *Exposition Internationale des Arts Décoratifs et Industriels Modernes* held in Paris was instrumental in popularizing the Art Deco movement that took its name.[33] The government sponsored exhibition aimed at promoting French architecture, jewelry, furniture, and other decorative and applied arts in several cleverly designed pavilions, including foreign ones, that were located on the *Esplanade des Invalides* and represented everything from cities and regions to department stores. Within the exhibition, the Franco-Swiss architect Charles-Édouard Jeanneret, better known as Le Corbusier, designed the *Esprit Nouveau* pavilion (fig. 0.35) in collaboration with the French artist Amédée Ozenfant, emphasizing a move towards Purism in art and architecture, a philosophy that admired the beauty and purity of the form of ordinary, mass-produced objects, and a clear rejection of the exhibition's overall theme of decorative arts. Conceived as a stark white box with a covered outdoor terrace in which an existing tree rises through the roof through a circular cutout, and large glass windows, the pavilion contained within its interiors Purist works of art and commercial furniture. Shortly thereafter, Ludwig Mies van der Rohe designed the German pavilion for the *Exposició Internacional de Barcelona* in 1929 (fig. 0.36), a structure that contained simple planar walls and free-flowing space to represent the openness

Fig. 0.35 | Pavillon L'Esprit Nouveau, International Exhibition of Modern Decorative and Industrial Arts, Paris, France, 1925, Le Corbusier and Pierre Jeanneret, licensed under the Creative Commons Attribution-ShareAlike 3.0 license

Fig. 0.36 | Barcelona Pavilion, Barcelona, Spain, Mies Van der Rohe, 1929, photo by Ashley Pomeroy, licensed under the Creative Commons Attribution 3.0 Unported,

of the new German republic.[34] The structural columns and roof were separated from the space-defining elements allowing for free movement between interior and exterior. So compelling was this approach that it was quickly adopted to private residences resulting in such well-known pavilion houses such as Mies van de Rohe's Farnsworth House in Plano, IL (1949-50), and Philip Johnson's Glass House in New Canaan, CT (1949, fig. 0.37).

Within the last fifty years or so, pavilions have become much more commonly associated with residential garden structures designed primarily for leisurely use on any number of occasions. They can be found as free-standing poolside structures or even semi-enclosed coverings for indoor swimming and other related spa and leisure activities. Often, pavilions serve entertaining functions with associated living, kitchen, and dining spaces opening to a garden or hardscaped terrace. Pavilions can also serve as small garden structures, home-offices, or even artist studios with associated display areas. Finally, pavilions can function as simple places of retreat for rest and relaxation, as the benefits of health and well-being *(benessere)* are intimately tied to the appreciation of garden landscapes or the countryside in general. As a result, the modern garden pavilion is neither an elite nor utilitarian structure but rather an alluring architectural form that can be found throughout the world in a variety of different settings.

~

This book considers the architecture of three recently completed pavilions by Peter Zimmerman Architects on the gardens of a large private house on Philadelphia's Main Line, and the associated characteristics that accompany these beautifully conceived and carefully built structures. Located on a portion of what was once the extensive property of the Ardrossan Estate, an early twentieth-century Georgian Revival mansion by Horace Trumbauer, the new pavilions accompany one of the next generation of houses that can now be seen on the rolling hills of the historic manor. Like Alvise Cornaro, the owners who commissioned the pavilions have taken on the responsibility of maintaining the

Introduction

Fig. 0.37 | Glass House, New Canaan, CT, USA, Philip Johnson, 1949, photo by Carol M. Highsmith, Carol M. Highsmith Archive, Library of Congress, LC-DIG-highsm-04817

land and character of the property as serious patrons of art, architecture, and landscape. Yet these new buildings also enhance the landscape, providing richer experiences in closer connection to nature, celebrating in fresh and harmonious ways the property's extraordinary history and the family's desire to enjoy the simple pleasures of life outdoors.

Notes:

[1] *On the Art of Building in Ten Books*, trans. by Joseph Rykwert et al. (Cambridge, Mass., and London: MIT Press, 1988): 18.

[2] *La Vita Sobria*, ed. A. Di Benedetto (Milan: Editori Associati, 1991); and G. Fiocco, *Alvise Cornaro il suo tempo e le sue opere* (Venice: Neri Pozza Editore, 1965).

[3] Robert Tavernor, *Palladio and Palladianism* (London: Thames & Hudson, 2003): 22-3.

[4] On Cornaro's treatise, see: Fiocco, *Alvise Cornaro*, 155-67; and C. Semenzato, ed., "Trattato di architettura," in *Trattati* (Milan: Edizioni Il Polifilo, 1985), 77-113.

[5] "[I]o lauderò sempre più la fabrica onestamente bella, ma perfettamente commoda, che la bellissima et incommoda." ("Trattato", [Semenzato], 101).

[6] Anthony Rich, *A Dictionary of Roman and Greek Antiquities* (London: Longmans, 1890): 475.

[7] Ibid., 640 and 648.

[8] *Histories* VI, xxvii–xlii.

[9] *De architectura*, II, 1.

[10] Rich, *A Dictionary of Roman and Greek Antiquities*, 475.

[11] *Historia Augusta*, Severus Alexander LI.

[12] On Constantine's dream, see Eusebius, *Life of Constantine* I, 28-31.

[13] *Letters*, II, 17.

[14] Wei Ran, *Buddhist Buildings: The Architecture of Monasteries, Pagodas, and Stone Caves* (New York: CN Times Books, 2014): 122-25: and Qiao Yun et al, *Ancient Chinese Architecture* (Hong Kong and Beijing: Joint Publishing Company and the China Building Industry Press, 1982): 80-82.

[15] Neville Agnew, et al. *Cave Temples of Dunhuang: Buddhist Art on China's Silk Road* (Los Angeles, California: Getty Conservation Institute, 2016).

[16] Edwin T. Morris, *The Gardens of China: History, Art, and Meanings* (New York: Scribner, 1983).

[17] Robert Irwin, *The Alhambra* (Cambridge, Mass.: Harvard University Press, 2004).

[18] Gülru Necipoğlu, *Architecture, Ceremonial, and Power: The Topkapi Palace in the Fifteenth and Sixteenth Centuries* (Cambridge, Mass.: MIT Press, 1991): 184 ff.

[19] Donald Newton Wilber, *Persian Gardens and Garden Pavilions* (Washington, DC: Dumbarton Oaks, 1979).

[20] Francesco Colonna, *Hypnerotomachia Poliphili*, translated by Joscelyn Godwin (London: Thames & Hudson, 2005).

[21] Sebastiano Serlio, *Sebastiano Serlio on Architecture* II, trans. by Vaughan Hart and Peter Hicks (New Haven: Yale University Press, 2001), p. 388.

[22] Donata Battilotti, *The Villas of Palladio* (Milan: Electa, 1990).

[23] Op.cit., trans. by R. Tavernor and R. Schofield (Cambridge, Mass., and London: The MIT Press), 2001, II.12.46

[24] David R. Coffin, *The Villa in the Life of Renaissance Rome* (Princeton: Princeton University Press, 1979).

[25] Cyril Connolly and Jerome Zerbe, *Les Pavillons: French Pavilions of the Eighteenth Century* (New York: Macmillan, 1962); and Bernd H. Dams and Andrew Zega, *Pleasure Pavilions and Follies in the Gardens of the Ancien Régime* (Paris and New York: Flammarion, 1995).

[26] George Mott and Sally Sample Aall, *Follies and Pleasure Pavilions: England, Ireland, Scotland, Wales* (New York: Harry N. Abrams, 1989).

[27] Jane Brown, *The Omnipotent Magician: Lancelot 'Capability' Brown, 1716-1783* (London: Pimlico, 2012): 206.

[28] José Luis Sancho, *La arquitectura de los sitios reales: catálogo histórico de los palacios, jardines y patronatos reales del Patrimonio Nacional* (Madrid: Patrimonio Nacional, 1995).

[29] Francesco Canestrini and Maria Rosaria Iacono, *The English Garden at the Royal Palace of Caserta* (Naples: Electa Napoli, 2004).

[30] Miles David Samson, *Hut Pavilion Shrine: Architectural Archetypes in Mid-Century Modernism* (Farnham, Surrey and Burlington, VT: Ashgate, 2015).

[31] Auguste-Rosalie Bisson, C. Michelez, and Pierre Petit. *Exposition Universelle de Paris 1867* (1867).

[32] Gabriele Basilico, et al, *Pavilions and Gardens of Venice Biennale* (Rome: Contrasto, 2013).

[33] Victoria Charles, and Klaus H. Carl, *Art Deco* (New York: Parkstone Press International, 2013).

[34] George Dodds, *Building Desire: On the Barcelona Pavilion* (New York: Routledge, 2005).

Chapter One

The Ardrossan Estate

The house Trumbauer designed for the Montgomerys had no champagne basin. But modest it was not. The design was inspired by a house in Surrey that had been featured in *Country Life*, a British weekly read closely by country gentlemen, arrived or aspiring. The Montgomery house would have fifteen bedrooms, fifteen fireplaces, and accommodations for twelve servants … For interior decoration, the Montgomerys hired the London firm that had overhauled Buckingham Palace after the death of Queen Victoria (Janny Scott).[1]

Fig. 1.1 | Aerial drone view of the Ardrossan House, 2022.

Ardrossan is an early twentieth-century Georgian Revival mansion with landscaped grounds built by the legendary Philadelphia architect, Horace Trumbauer, on an expansive rolling site not far from Villanova, in the community of Radnor Township, Pennsylvania (fig. 1.2).[2] The area, known colloquially as the Main Line because of its railway connection to the city, was home to some of the most extraordinary country estates of the region belonging to the wealthiest families of Philadelphia.[3] Originally built and continuously maintained to this day by the Montgomery family, the story of Ardrossan is one of architecture, estate management, and of course Philadelphia society. The name Ardrossan comes from a small town on the North Ayrshire coast of Scotland where the Montgomery's ancestors resided before coming to America. The name in Gaelic means "high small promontory" which is appropriate as the house sits on a knoll about half a mile south of Newtown Road (fig. 1.1), a historic southwest route that was laid in 1724 and connected the Radnor Meeting Hall with the Church in New Town.[4] The Meeting House was located in village of Radnorville (now Ithan), and the two names also had Gaelic origins, as the Ithon River runs through the mid Wales district of Radnorshire, the region from which the earliest settlers of Radnor Township arrived.[5]

There are many myths and legends related to the foundation of the Ardrossan estate but without question equestrian sport was an essential factor, as the young Robert Montgomery, the man who eventually acquired the property and built the great house, was familiar with the terrain as he frequently rode his horse across the site with the Radnor Hunt, a fox chase established in 1883.[6] Between 1908 and 1910, Colonel Montgomery (as he was later called) purchased 309 acres south of Newtown Road which bordered the old Radnor Hunt (figs. 1.3-4). In 1911, he began building the massive family mansion which was modeled on an English country house named Ardenrun Place designed by the British architect, Ernest Newton, and located in the countryside of Blindley Heath, Surrey.[7] The new family estate would be home to Colonel Montgomery and Charlotte Hope Binney Tyler, his wife, their four children, Mrs. Montgomery's aunt, several generations of grandchildren, and many domestic staff. Yet Ardrossan was more than simply a large family home, the property looked out over a pastoral landscape that served as pastureland for the family's prized Ayrshire dairy cattle, Shropshire sheep, and of course horses. Dairy barns, stables, workmen's cottages, garages, a gate-lodge, and water tower were among the many additional buildings that were scattered across the estate - many of which were designed or renovated by the Philadelphia partnership of Louis S. Adams and A. Chandler Manning - making it a truly English-inspired country house.

Fig. 1.2 | Colonel Montgomery's Ardrossan Estate from the south-east, photographed 09-02-1939, Collection ID: 70_200_12164, J. Victor Dallin Aerial Survey Collection (Accession 1970.200), Audiovisual Collections I Digital Initiatives Dept., Hagley Museum & Library, Wilmington, DE 19807. Photo restoration by Phil Graham 2022.

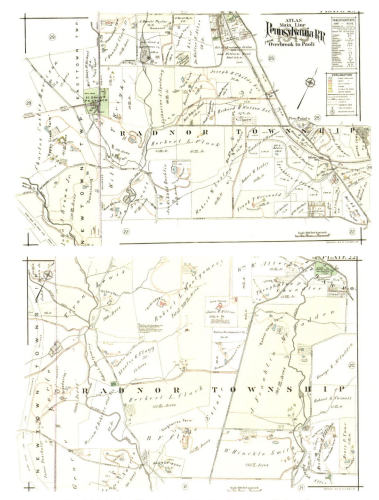

Figs. 1.3-4 | Atlas of Properties on Main Line Pennsylvania Railroad from Overbrook to Paoli, 1913 – Plate 22. Creator: A. H. Mueller, Publisher. Scan restoration by Phil Graham 2022. | Atlas of Properties on Main Line Pennsylvania Railroad from Overbrook to Paoli, 1913 – Plate 23. Creator: A.H. Mueller, Publisher. Scan restoration by Phil Graham 2022.

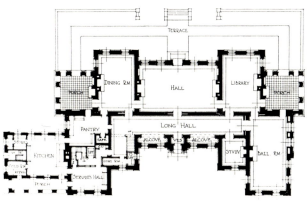

Fig. 1.5 | Simplified floorplan of Ardrossan showing minor 1912 revisions to the service wing. Source: Radnor Historical Society.

The main house is a stretched "H" in plan with the main entry façade facing north and the garden façade south (fig. 1.5). There is an additional service wing with a porch added to the northeast corner of the house and two semi-enclosed pavilions flanking the southern façade that are used as morning and afternoon entertainment porches. The main entrance consists of a two-story limestone frontispiece with the lower floor portal articulated by attached Corinthian columns and the central window above framed by carved garlanded herms supporting a simple and elegant cornice and iron balcony. In plan, the ground floor has a series of formal rooms facing south that include a dining room adjacent to the service wing, a great central hall with fireplaces on the end walls, and a library for late-afternoon relaxation. These rooms all open onto a garden terrace that overlooks the pastoral landscape. The north side contains an entry vestibule which leads to a long picture gallery with alcoves on either side of

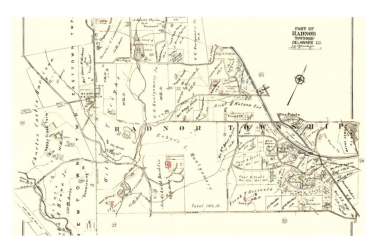

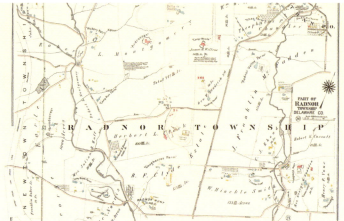

Figs. 1.6-7 | Atlas of Properties on Main Line Pennsylvania Railroad from Overbrook to Paoli, 1926 – Plate 22. Creator: George W. & Walter S. Bromley. Publisher: G.W. Bromley & Co. Source: Julieann G. Shanahan collection. Scan restoration by Phil Graham 2022. | Atlas of Properties on Main Line Pennsylvania Railroad from Overbrook to Paoli, 1926 – Plate 22. Creator: George W. & Walter S. Bromley. Publisher: G.W. Bromley & Co. Source: Julieann G. Shanahan collection. Scan restoration by Phil Graham 2022.

Fig. 1.8 | Aerial photo taken 12.1.1937 over Wayne, PA, 19085. Source: DVPRC, State of New Jersey, Esri, HERE, Garmin, GeoTechnologies, Inc., USGS, METI/NASA, EPA, USDA. Photo restoration by Phil Graham.

the entrance, a great open stair towards the service wing, and a ballroom and small study at the opposite end by the library. The bedrooms, guest suites, and service quarters are all located on the upper two floors of which the third is in the attic and illuminated by large Palladian inspired dormers, and a series of intricately carved roundels within the tympanum of the end gables of the roof. Built of exposed brick, with limestone detailing, sash windows, a simple cornice, and a slate tile roof with eleven large projecting chimneys, the house - though discreet in appearance - could easily fit in any of the southern counties of England.

Colonel Montgomery continued to buy adjacent properties increasing the size of the original estate from just over 300 acres in 1913 to 542 acres in 1920, largely through the acquisition of lands north of Newtown Road (figs. 1.6-7). In 1922, the family made their last major land acquisition, buying 200 acres of the Tryon Lewis estate on the south side of Newtown Road, bringing their total land holding to 752 acres (fig. 1.8). Of the many expansions, three north of Newtown Road are particularly relevant.[8] The first was the purchase of 60 acres of the Robert W. Lesley estate on July 10, 1916, that included the Orchard Lodge, a 1720 stone farmhouse that with several renovations would become an extended family residence for the Montgomerys, and the other was the acquisition of the Herbert L. Clark estate in 1920, a property that was referred to as the Watson Farm or Field, consisting of 86 acres. This latter site is where the Montgomerys converted the Watson Barn into Ardrossan's Dairy No. 3. The third site, a 25-acre lot belonging to Mrs. William Henry Sayen just south of Church Road and east of the Clark estate, was acquired by Colonel Montgomery in March 1929 primarily for an existing five-bay, two-and-a-half-story house called Aeola that sat on the property. The Colonel renamed it Hopelands, after his daughter Helen Hope Montgomery Scott (fig. 1.9), and Horace Trumbauer subsequently renovated it in 1930 as a wedding present for Hope and future family heirs.[9]

Several historic images' show the site north of Newtown Road in its original condition with the barn in the distance, sheep grazing on the fields, or during a chase with foxhounds, horses, and their respective riders "coffee housing" during the hunt (figs. 1.10-14).[10] The American painter, Charles Morris Young, a resident of Radnor and sport painter of golf, equestrian, and hunting scenes, produced some of his most renowned landscape paintings at Ardrossan.[11] One painting titled *Montgomery's Meadow* from 1927 captured the character of the site on a chilly grey chase day, with rolling fields in the foreground, wooded clusters in the middle, and distant hills in the background (fig. 1.15).[12] For the most part,

Fig. 1.9 | Helen Hope Montgomery Scott c.1985-90 with her dog "Bander". Originally published in the Suburban & Wayne Times (n.d.). View looking approx. SE from Church Rd towards Newtown Rd. on skyline. House on left is Hope & Edgar Scott's Orchard Lodge. Source: Radnor Historical Society. Photo restoration by Phil Graham.

Fig. 1.10 | View northward across an area known by the Montgomerys as the Watson Farm, believed to have been formerly rented by Richard H. Watson whose personal estate was on the north side of Church Road. Source: Montgomery-Scott-Wheeler family collection. Photo restoration by Phil Graham 2022.

Fig. 1.11 | View of "The Watson Farm" (Ardrossan's Dairy #3) towards SE from Church Rd. Source: Montgomery-Scott-Wheeler family collection. Photo restoration by Phil Graham 2022.

Fig. 1.13 | "Working horses with Howard & Joe Fair. August 1939. Showing horses going both ways across street." Photo later appeared in April 1940 Country Life article, "Conditioning Hunters", written by Howard Fair, with the caption: "Galloping over rough going, a young hunter learns to watch his footing." Montgomery-Scott-Wheeler family collection. Photo restoration by Phil Graham.

Fig. 1.12 | Hand-written caption reads, "Watson sheep", from a series of photos dated 1899. Photo shows sheep grazing on "The Watson Farm" - precise location undetermined. Source: Radnor Historical Society. Photo restoration by Phil Graham 2022.

Fig. 1.14 | "Double Entry", taken for the "Philadelphia Record", Metropolitan Section, Sunday, September 15, 1946. Caption: "PRETTY FACES: In the oval on her Villanova estate, Mrs. Edgar Scott (left) watches a parade of horse show entries. In the lineup are Miss Virginia Montgomery, Edgar Scott, Jr., Miss Cassandra Cassatt, Miss Lalla Smith and Alexander Cassatt, Jr., The hounds also look interested." Montgomery-Scott-Wheeler family collection. Photo restoration by Phil Graham.

the land has changed very little since then, which brings us to the present story.

As previously noted, Ardrossan remains in the hands of the Montgomery family, though over the years, sections of the estate have been sold off for speculative development, especially the land north of Newtown Road. In 1997, the Montgomery family sold off 172.5 acres of the Ardrossan Farm north of Newtown Road, subdivided into 17 lots including the Orchard Lodge, to be used for residential or agricultural purposes.[13] The local Brandywine Conservancy conservation easement stipulated that the 17 lots could be further consolidated into 10 parcels with no further subdivisions except for minor line adjustments. Between 1998 and 2001, the Villanova architect, Fred L. Bissinger, designed a traditional stone house on Lot #3, an 8.5-acre parcel of the Watson Farm across the street from the remaining Ardrossan estate with direct access from Newtown Road almost opposite the Horace Trumbauer designed entry gate to the historic house (fig. 1.16). The owners of the new parcel wanted a Cotswold-style country cottage even though the architect had a high regard for Ardrossan's Georgian plan and appearance. The result was an interesting hybrid house that adopted an "H" plan for the main volume and a more cottage-like butterfly extension to the north and a free-standing garage structure just beyond (fig. 1.17). Yet unlike the brick exterior of Ardrossan, the new house was clad in local field stone giving it a much more rustic character (fig. 1.18). An aerial perspective sketch of the house produced by the architect shows the expansive structure resting on an open knoll with the circular entry forecourt viewed from the east and a free-standing stone pavilion in the garden to the south (fig. 1.19). That structure was eventually built though regrettably the stone pavilion was never realized. The new owners did plant two rows of Pear Blossom trees (29 in total) to line the gravel drive from Newtown Road to the entry court, making the first significant change to the historic agricultural landscape (fig. 1.20).

Fig. 1.15 | "Montgomery's Meadow" by Charles Morris Young. Photographed by Tom Crane. Painting in the Montgomery-Scott-Wheeler family collection. Color matching/restoration by Phil Graham.

In early 2016, the new house was sold to the present owners who immediately set off on renovating the house to meet its growing family's needs, and to build upon the strengths of the existing house and historic landscape. The owners hired the local architect, Peter Zimmerman, known for his traditional residential work on both new houses and renovations and additions. The first project consisted of renovating the interiors of the existing Bissinger designed house, transforming the main hall just off the entrance by giving it a more classicizing character, more in line with much of the detailing already present in the fireplace

Fig. 1.16 | Aerial drone view of the Shanahan Property, © Jeffrey Totaro, 2022

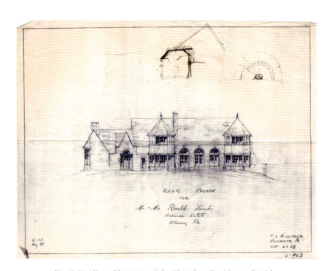

Fig. 1.18 | Rear Elevation of the Shanahan Residence, Fred L. Bissinger Architect, May 1998.

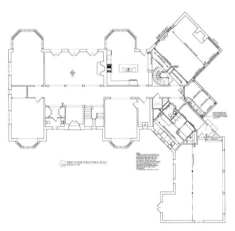

Fig. 1.17 | Plan of the Shanahan Residence, Peter Zimmerman Architects, 2016. This is the original H plan by Fred Bissinger with Zimmerman's alterations for the Shanahan family.

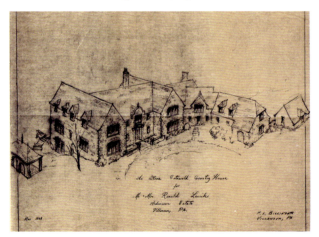

Fig. 1.19 | Aerial Perspective Drawing of the Shanahan Residence, Fred L. Bissinger Architect, May 1998.

surround, the two free-standing Doric columns and attendant pilasters that separate the hall from the entry vestibule, and the three large arched doorways equally framed by Doric pilasters, giving access to the upper garden terrace (figs. 1.21-22). The new design transformed the Doric columns into square piers and the arched doorways into rectangular casement doors in line with windows elsewhere on the house, closed off an upper story open balcony, and provided more classically canonical cornices and moldings throughout. This was followed by reconfiguring the front doorway which the new owners did not particularly like. The original door was a projecting arched aedicule with a scallop shell in the segmental volume above the solid panel doors. The new design provided glazed doors to allow for greater light inside, and a flat metal rib and frame grill in the lunette under the arch with translucent glass behind and a family crest in the center (figs. 1.23). With these two simple renovations, a more direct axis could be made visible through the center of the house connecting the entry forecourt with the vestibule, main hall, and upper garden terrace at the back (fig. 1.24).

The owners also demolished a fan-shaped glazed sunroom that filled the gap between the two butterfly extensions to the north, replacing it with a covered porch, and renovated the double-height family room that occupied the western wing of the split wedge. Working closely with an interior designer, the owners also had most of the public rooms - especially the main hall, dining room and pantry - given highly individual treatments that when seen together culminate in a bold and daring combination of fabrics, wall coverings, floor treatments, and furniture, as if the rustic Cotswold-style cottage were the perfect ground for design invention, fancy, and creative contemporary expression (figs. 1.25-26).

The next set of renovations took place in the basement overlooking the lower garden terrace where a new pool was under construction, and two free-standing pavilions would eventually be built. Here the architects transformed the existing area to provide a new informal living room off the

Fig. 1.20 | View of the Entry Drive lined with Pear Blossom Trees, © Stacey Fitzpatrick Photography, April 22, 2018.

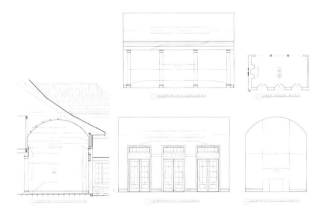

Fig. 1.21 | Main Hall renovations, plan, sections, and elevations by Peter Zimmerman Architects, © 2016.

Fig. 1.22 | Interior View of the Main Hall. © Jeffrey Totaro, 2022.

lower garden terrace with a kitchenette, cabana bath, laundry facility, and bunk room for the children's guests (fig. 1.27). The new spaces could be accessed directly from the main staircase to the right of the entry vestibule as one entered the house, and in doing so, offer visitors two distinct spatial sequences as one arrived, a more formal axial path to the main hall and upper terrace, or a more informal descent to the underground pool area. With the house in order, it was time for the new owners to tackle the property's historic landscape. The parcel consisted of a trapezoidal lot oriented southeast to northwest, approximately 500 ft. inland from Newtown Road (fig. 1.28). As already noted, the site was accessed by a 50 ft. wide gravel drive lined with Pear Blossom trees that extended from Newtown Road to the large circular entry court fronting the house. The gravel drive and house rested on the highest part of the property and the land descended from there in all directions. A wooded stream called Abraham's Run, named in honor of Isaac Abrahams

Fig. 1.23 | Front Entrance renovation, sketch drawing by Peter Zimmerman Architects, © 2017.

The Ardrossan Estate

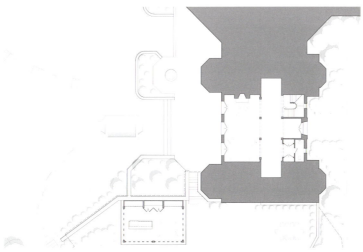

Fig. 1.24 | Plan View of the entry sequence from the Circular Forecourt, through the Entry Vestibule and Main Hall, to the Upper Terrace Garden, drawing by Peter Zimmerman Architects, © 2022.

Fig. 1.25 | Interior View of the Dining Room Pantry, © Jeffrey Totaro, 2022.

Fig. 1.26 | Interior View of the Entry Vestibule, © Jeffrey Totaro, 2022.

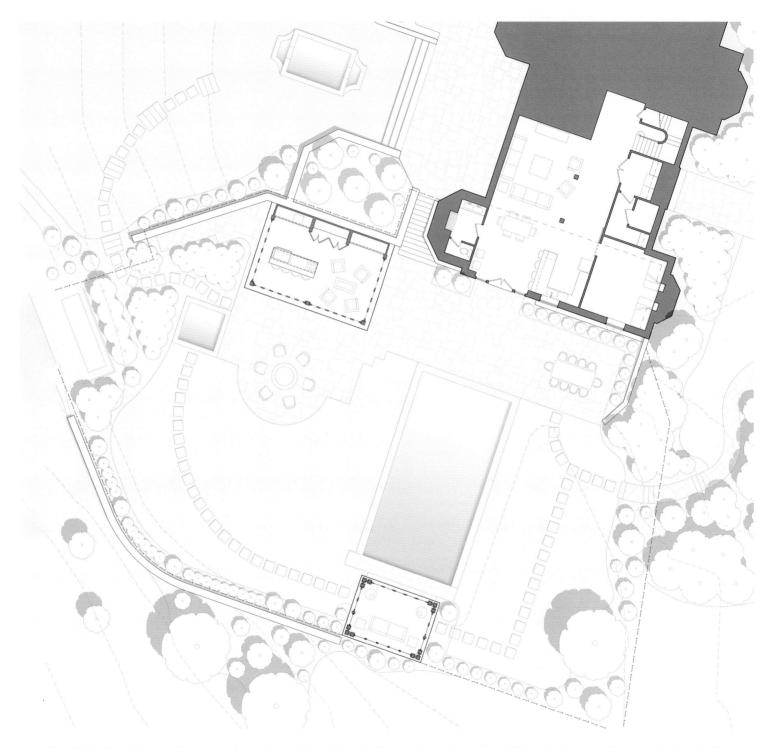

Fig. 1.27 | Plan View of the ground floor sequence from the Main Stair, through the Family Room, to the Lower Terrace Pool and Garden, drawing by Peter Zimmerman Architects, © 2022.

Fig. 1.28 | Brandywine Conservancy Conservation Easement, Subdivision Plan prepared by Momenee and Associates, Inc., October 6, 1997

Fig. 1.29 | Front Gate, sketch drawing by Peter Zimmerman Architects, © 2019.

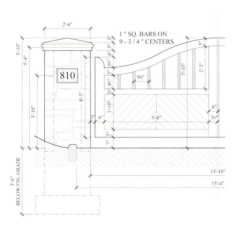

Fig. 1.30 | Front Gate (detail), sketch drawing by Peter Zimmerman Architects, © 2019.

Fig. 1.31 | View of the Front Gate, © Jeffrey Totaro, 2022

and weeds, and tick infested. The owners working with the Brandywine Conservancy inventoried the indigenous, non-indigenous, and landscape planted trees to determine what needed to remain and what could be removed. The clearing of the woodland also included the removal of decades of refuse that had accumulated by the stream, and medicinally treating several Ash trees to stave off Emerald Ash Borer disease (fig. 1.32). The land maintenance and rejuvenation remain ongoing projects that preserve the landscape as both a historical and pastoral backdrop to the new pavilions that the owners eventually built throughout the property, and which occupy the next several chapters of this book (fig. 1.33).

Notes:
[1] Janny Scott, *The Beneficiary: Fortune, Misfortune, and the Story of My Father* (New York: Riverhead Books, 2019): 39.
[2] David Nelson Wren, *Ardrossan: The Last Great Estate on the Philadelphia Main Line* (New York: Bauer and Dean Publishers, 2018); and Michael C. Kathrens, *American Splendor: The Residential Architecture of Horace Trumbauer* (New York: Acanthus Press, 2002): 183-90.
[3] Katharine Hewitt Cummin, *A Rare and Pleasing Thing: Radnor Demography* (1798) and *Development* (Philadelphia: Owlswick Press, 1977); John W. Jordan, *A History of Delaware County, Pennsylvania, and Its People*, 2 Vols. (New York: Lewis Historical Publishing Company, 1914); Samuel T. Wiley and Winfield Scott Garner, *Biographical and Historical Cyclopedia of Delaware County, Penn.: Comprising a Historical Sketch of the County* (Richmond, IN: Gresham Pub. Co., 1894); Henry Graham Ashmead and Austin N. Hungerford, *History of Delaware County, Pennsylvania* (Philadelphia: L.H. Everts, 1884); and George Smith, *History of Delaware County, Pennsylvania from the Discovery of the Territory Included Within its Limits to the Present Time: With a Notice of the Geology of the County, and Catalogues of its Minerals, Plants, Quadrupeds and Birds* (Philadelphia: H.B. Ashmead, 1862).
[4] Chester County Archive, "NewtownRoadRadnorPa_1725-02-22_ChesterCoPaArchives-road-docket-A1_1686-1724."
[5] Jordan, A *History of Delaware County*, vol. 1, 309-10; and Wiley and Garner, *Biographical and Historical Cyclopedia of Delaware County*, 141.
[6] On the Radnor Hunt, see Collin F. McNeil, *Bright Hunting Morn: The 125th Anniversary of the Radnor Hunt* (New York: The Derrydale Press, 2009).
[7] Lawrence Weaver, "Ardenrun Place," *Country Life* (January 21, 1911): 90-96.
[8] Cummin, *A Rare and Pleasing Thing*, 164-86.
[9] The house is still in the family, see Scott, *The Beneficiary*, 62-63; and Wren, *Ardrossan*, 263-64.
[10] When people are chattering instead of paying attention, see http://www.harvardfoxhounds.com/HFH_Fox_Hunting_Terms.html
[11] Wren, *Ardrossan*, 190-94; Mantle Fielding, *Dictionary of American Painters, Sculptors and Engravers*, ed. by Genevieve C. Doran (Greens Farms, Conn.: Modern Books and Crafts, 1974): 421; and McNeil, *Bright Hunting Morn*, 151.
[12] The painting is dated March 20, 1927 and was acquired by Colonel Montgomery in 1936. See Wren, *Ardrossan*, 190.
[13] Brandywine Conservancy, "Conservation Easement and Declaration of Restrictions and Covenants" (October 6, 1997).

Fig. 1.32 | The Author and Owner discussing the land maintenance and rejuvenation above Abraham's Run, © Jeffrey Totaro, 2022

who owned a portion of the land in the early 19th century and ran it as a farm, defined a large portion of the northwest edge of the site.[14] The owners commissioned Peter Zimmerman to design a new entry gate set back slightly from Newtown Road to provide a more formal entry to the property and frame the stunning allée of Pear Blossom trees (figs. 1.29-31). A simple set of curved wooden farm gates with panels below and rails above, were held by two 30" by 30" stone piers topped with limestone caps. Stone pavers connected the entry gate to Newtown Road at one end and the gravel drive at the other, adding to the rustic yet formal quality of the entry sequence.

The biggest challenge, as previously noted, was taming, and pruning the woodland by Abraham's Run which was overrun with tangled brush

Fig. 1.33 | New Site Plan, drawing by Peter Zimmerman Architects, © 2022.

Chapter Two

Pool Pavilion

~

Pool Pavilion Iso

Pool Pavilion

Pool Pavilion Iso

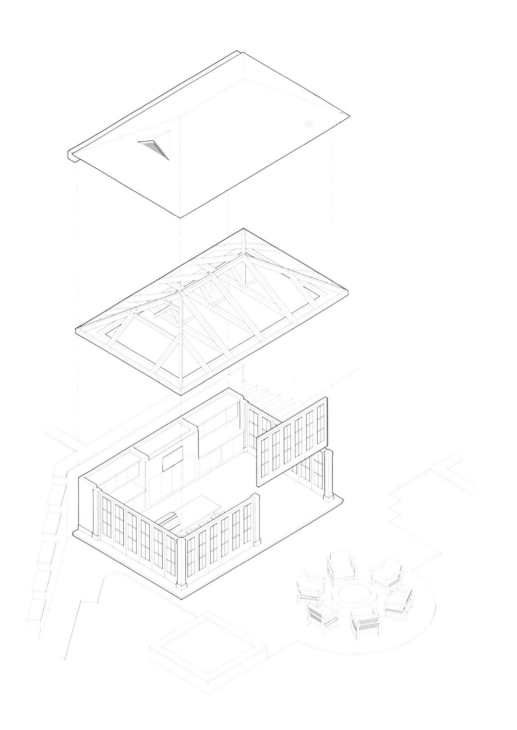

Pool Pavilion Exploded Axon

Pool Pavilion

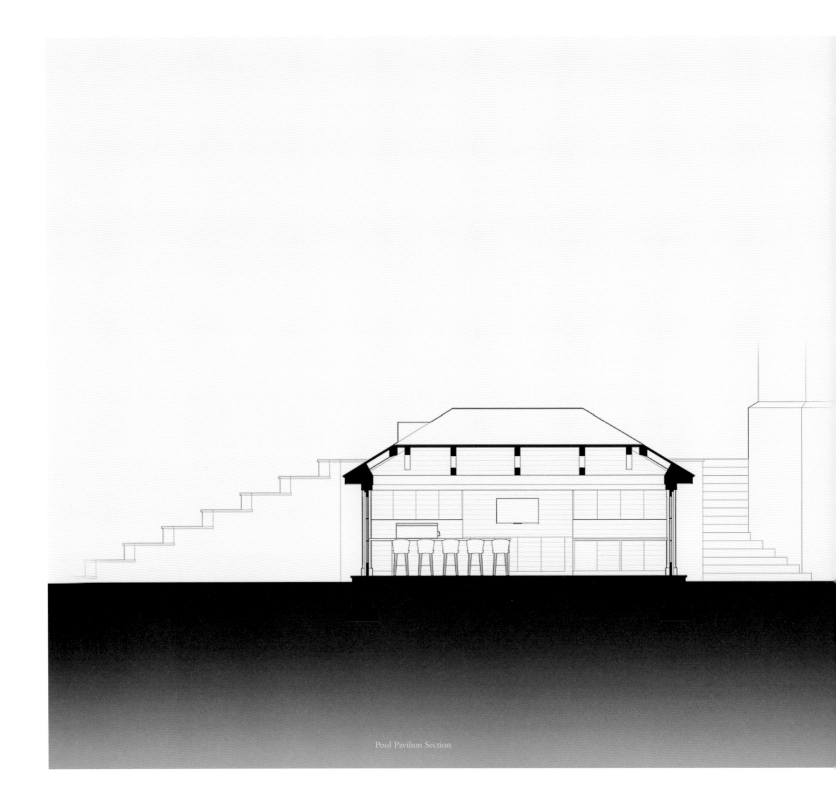
Pool Pavilion Section

Pool Pavilion

Pool Pavilion Section

Pool Pavilion

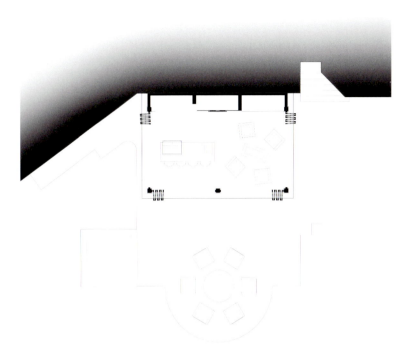

Pool Pavilion Floor Plan

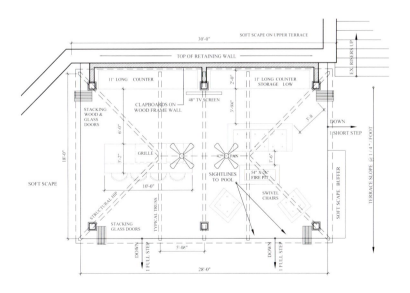

Pool Pavilion Plan

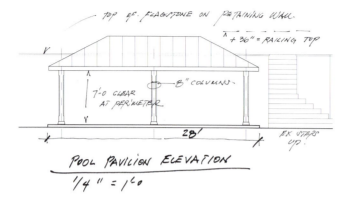

Pool Pavilion Elevation

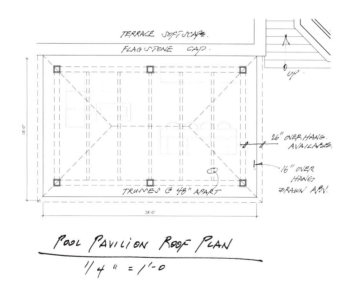

Pool Pavilion Roof Plan

Pool Pavilion

Pool Pavilion

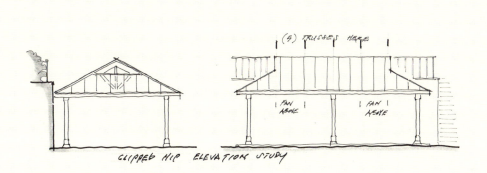

Clipped Hip Elevation Study

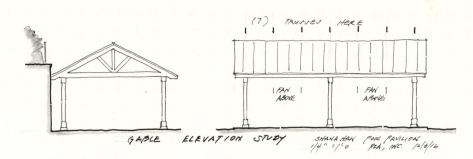

Gable Elevation Study

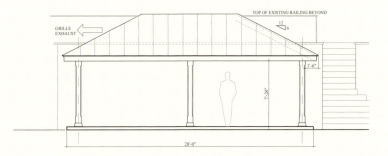

Pool Pavilion Elevation

Pool Pavilion

Pool Pavilion

Pool Pavilion

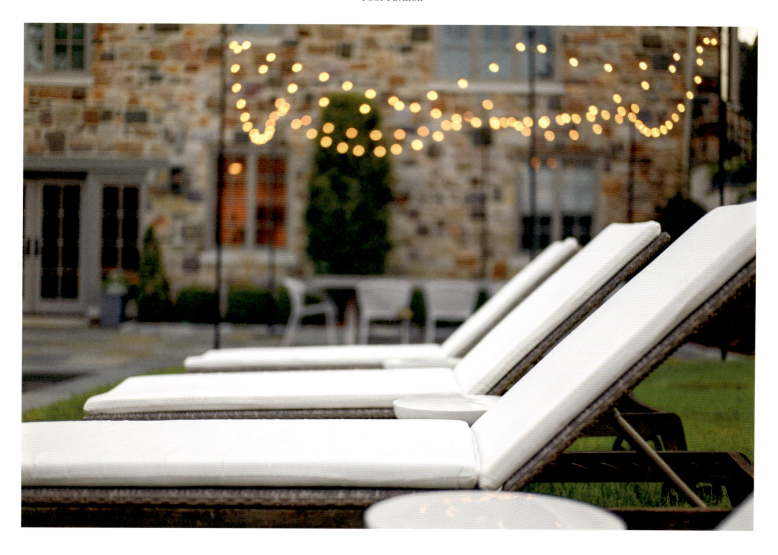

Pool Pavilion

Construction

Pool Pavilion

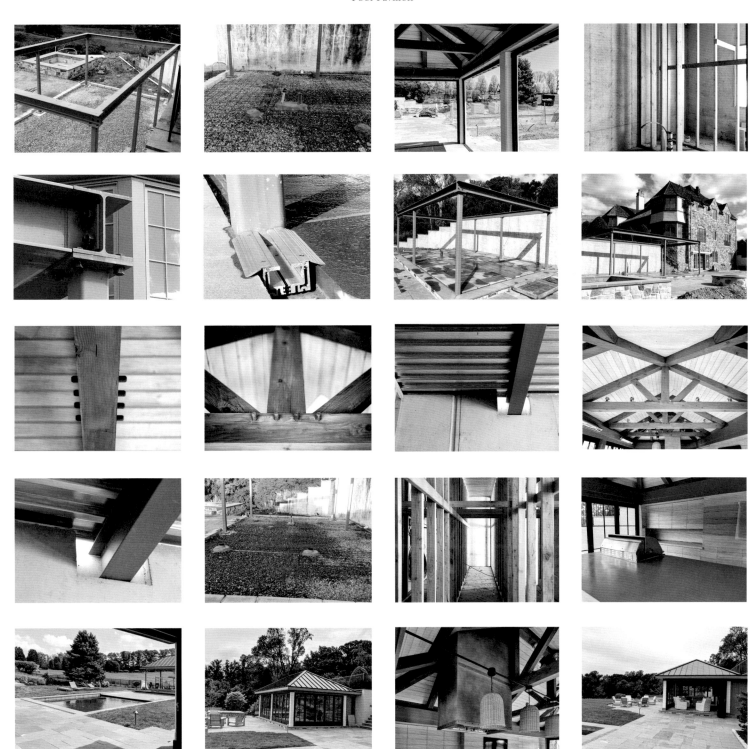

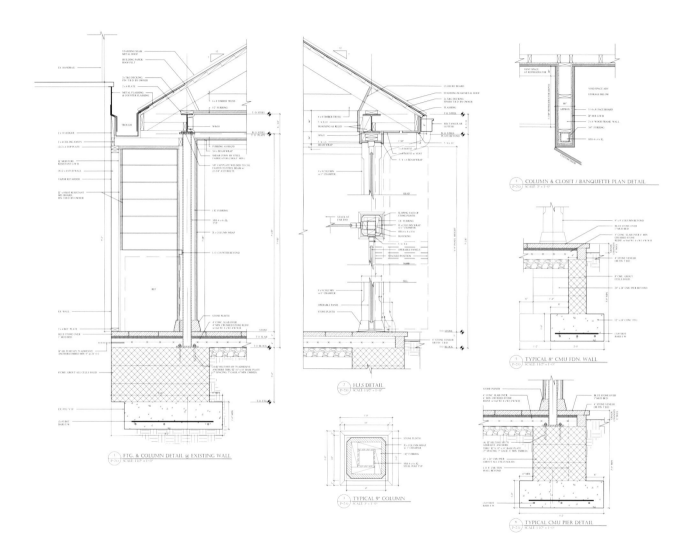

Pool Pavilion Working Drawings

Pool Pavilion

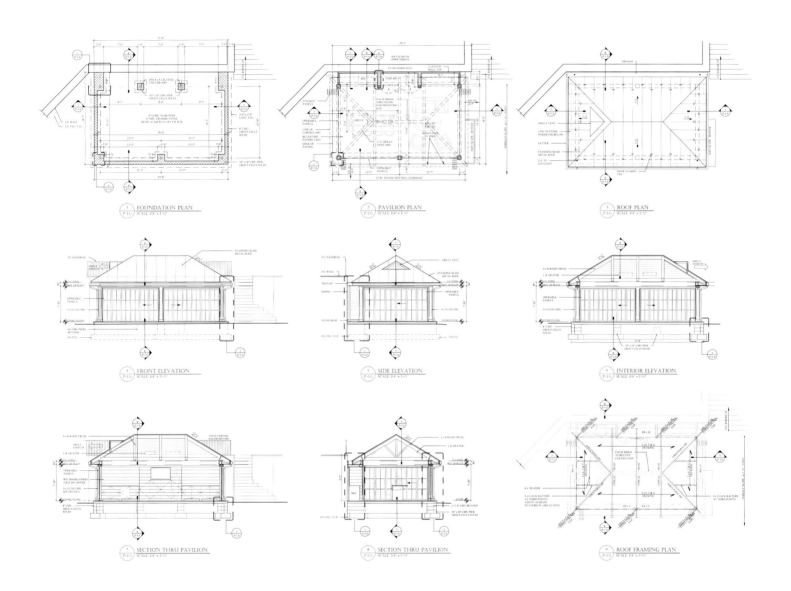

Pool Pavilion Working Drawings

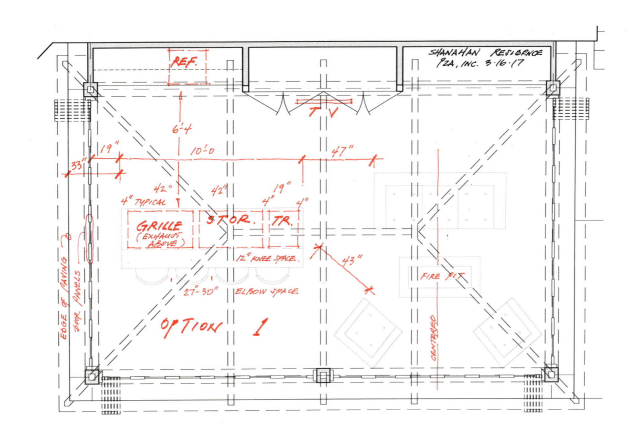

Pool Pavilion Plan

Chapter Three

Pool Cabana

~

Pool Cabana Iso

Pool Cabana

Pool Cabana Iso

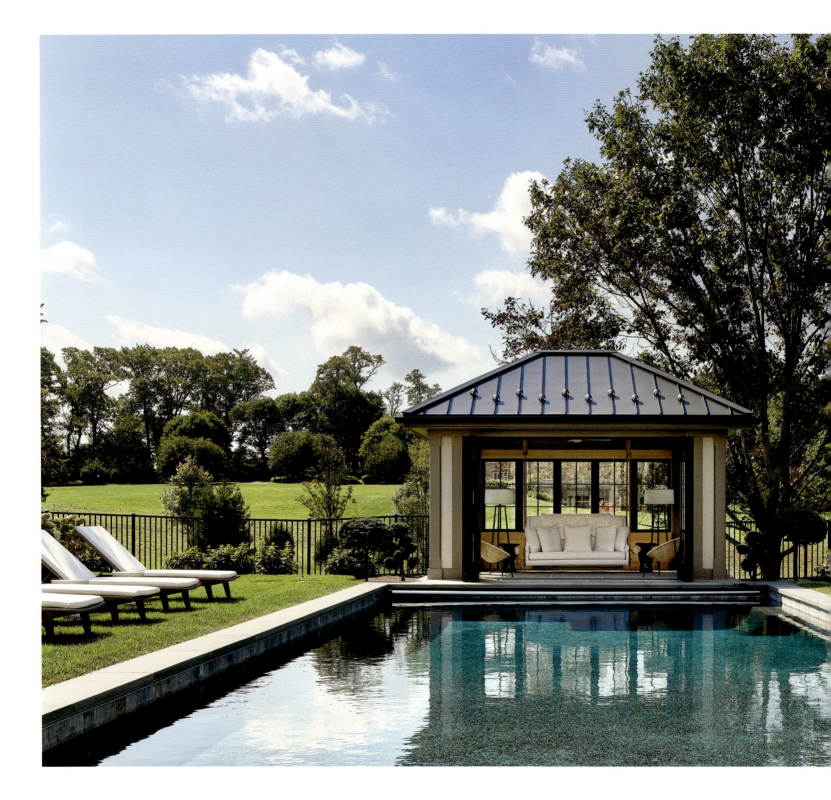

Pool Cabana

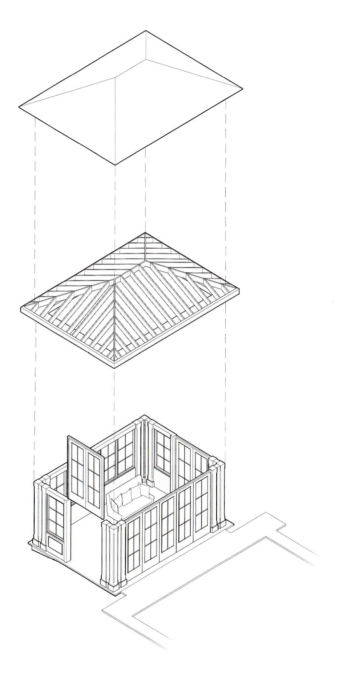

Pool Cabana Exploded Axon

Pool Cabana Sections

Pool Cabana

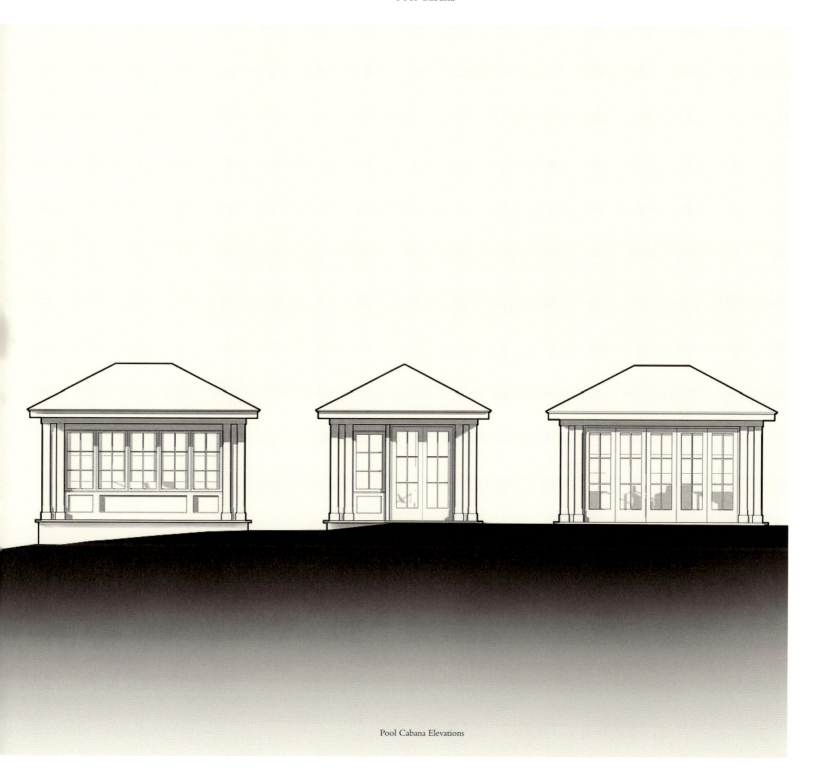

Pool Cabana Elevations

Pool Cabana

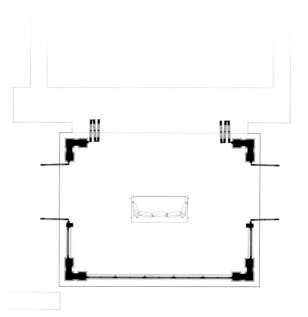

Pool Cabana Floor Plan

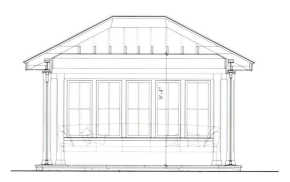

Pool Cabana Section

Pool Cabana

Pool Cabana

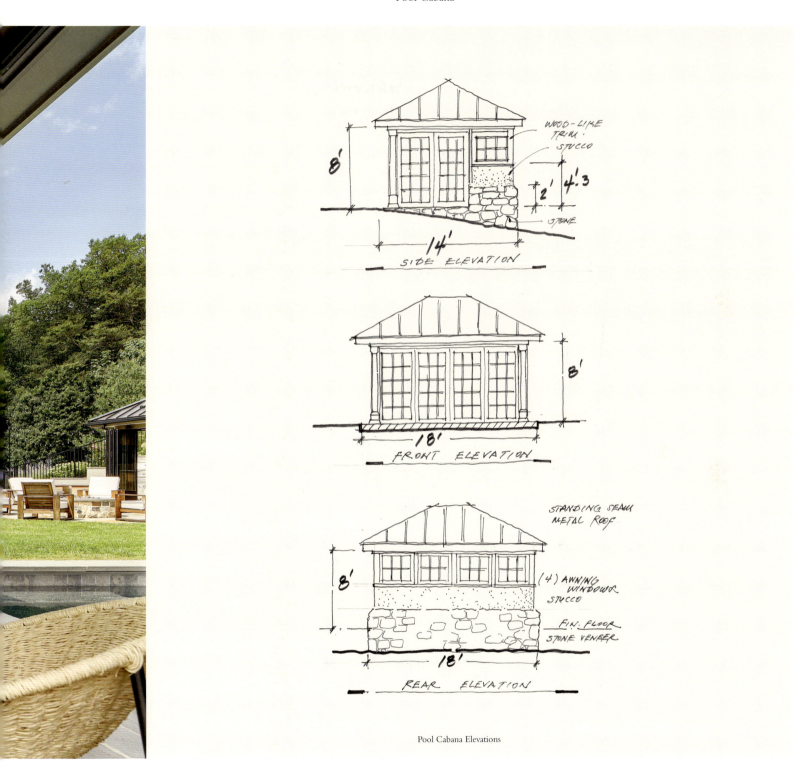

Pool Cabana Elevations

Pool Cabana

Pool Cabana

Pool Cabana

Construction

Pool Cabana

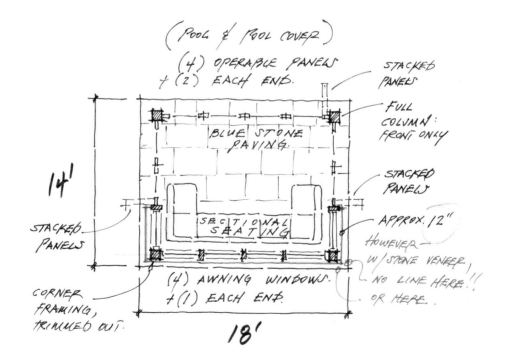

Pool Cabana Plan

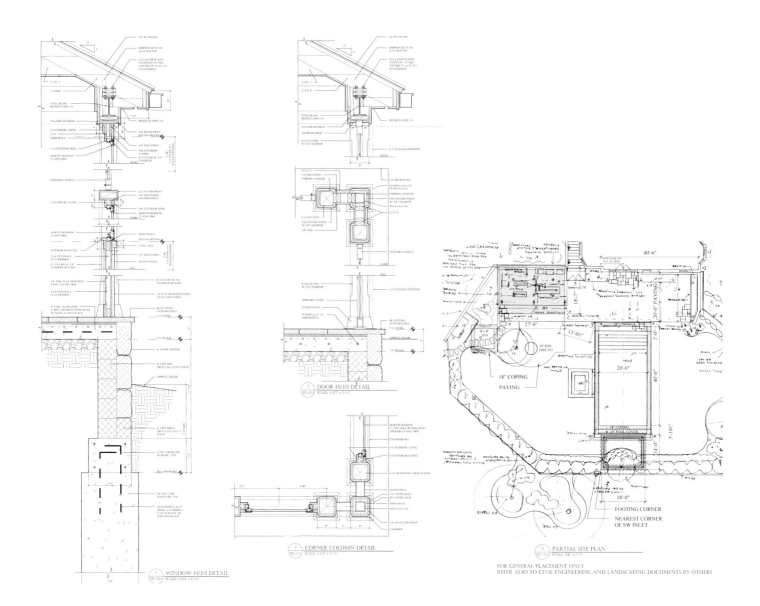

Pool Cabana Working Drawings

Pool Cabana

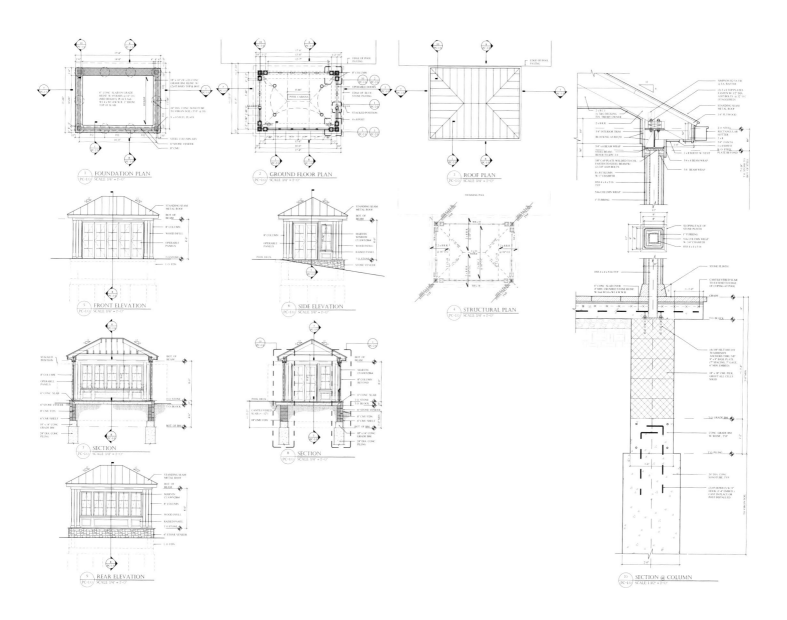

Pool Cabana Working Drawings

Chapter Four

Ashwood Run

∿

Because of the discovery of fire, there arose at the beginning, concourse among men, deliberation and a life in common … observing the houses of others and adding to their ideas new things from day to day, they produced better kinds of huts … with upright forked props and twigs put between, they wove their walls. Others made walls, drying moistened clods which they bound with wood, and covered with reeds and leafage, so as to escape the rain and heat. When in winter-time the roofs could not withstand the rains, they made ridges, and smearing clay down the sloping roofs, they drew off the rain-water (Vitruvius, *De architectura*, Bk. II, chap. 1).

If the Pool Pavilion and Cabana are places for experiencing and enjoying daily events such as eating and drinking, conversing with family and friends, or relaxing in private by the pool, then the Ashwood Run pavilion is certainly a place for special events and celebrations, catering to the kinds of things that don't occur every day. Separated from the house and lower garden area and placed on the sloping edge of a stream and forest, named Ashwood Run for the creek that lies at its base, the new pavilion seems to grow out of the woods, recalling Vitruvius' legendary tale of the first primitive hut or cabin in the woods. But its placement in the landscape is deliberate, a terminal focus of the more formal sequence of spaces that run through the house and upper garden. From the front door, one moves into the vestibule and the view opens as you pass through the great hall, and from there the Ashwood Run pavilion emerges from the landscape. By situating the structure against the tree line and obliquely to the direct line of sight from the house, the structure activates what was once an unusable portion of the 8-acre site as a kind of garden folly.

In fact, the pavilion originally began as a small playhouse nestled against the backdrop of the tree line but grew into a larger 750 square foot cabin with multiple floors including a secret belvedere treehouse, complete with ladder and hatch. The main floor contains a great fieldstone fireplace near the center with three open sides for gathering and socializing around it. A large open dining space in front of the fireplace can accommodate a long table for up to 20 guests, whereas the two shorter sides include more intimate seating areas and a small wet bar. Behind the fireplace, and directly beneath the secret treehouse, is a small private bathroom that faces the woods. The treehouse is located within the pavilions steeply pitched roof, providing intimate views into the woods and of course the stream below which the owners made much more visible through their careful land maintenance and rejuvenation projects. The sloping site also made it possible to have an ample basement level with a small outdoor terrace enclosed by a stone wall and accessed from a wraparound staircase at the side. The basement space includes a professionally

designed catering kitchen, a large dog bath, and abundant storage space, whereas the terrace contains an outdoor barbeque smoker and grill. Nearby in the woods, is another stone fire pit for socializing, watching butterflies, or simply relaxing in privacy.

If the poolside pavilions are light and tent-like in character, then the Ashwood Run pavilion is a heavy-timber and stone hut with a steeply pitched roof that is rustic in character and detailing. Placed on a bluestone plinth and enclosed with folding glass windows, the slightly rectangular structure rises on twelve heavy piers that support a steeply pitched hip-and-gable roof clad in red cedar shakes and punctuated by front and back dormers and side vents. The central piers at the front and back are coupled to maintain the symmetrical distribution throughout and to emphasize the main orientation of the structure. The front dormer provides additional light to the double-height main space, whereas the rear dormer projects on heavy wood brackets adding extra space to the treehouse. The interior detailing is of red oak and the exposed roof reveals the extraordinary carpentry work of the massive roof trusses with mortise and tenon joinery. A series of X-braced wood panels bookend the four corners at the base adding to the structure's artful timber work in general.

As noted by the architect Peter Zimmerman, "[i]n Ashwood, timeless natural materials have been coupled with sophisticated amenities to create something at the woods' edge that is both a complete backyard venue for gatherings and a perfect reason to trek out to a previously seldom used portion of the estate." When seen in tandem with its two other sibling pavilions, the Ashwood Run structure appears to stand confidently in the landscape, seemingly independent as if from a separate world. Yet the combination of wood, stone, and shingle recalls the Cotswold-like character of the main house, completing the tripartite structure of butterflies, tents, and wooden huts that make up this extraordinary historic property.

Ashwood Run Isos

Ashwood Run

Ashwood Run Isos

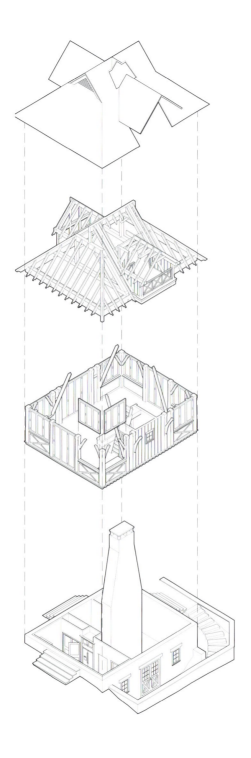

Ashwood Run Exploded Axon

Ashwood Run

Ashwood Run

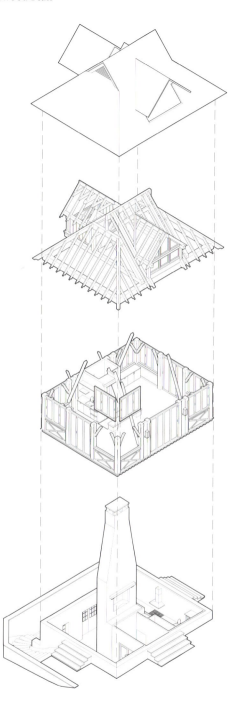

Ashwood Run Exploded Axon

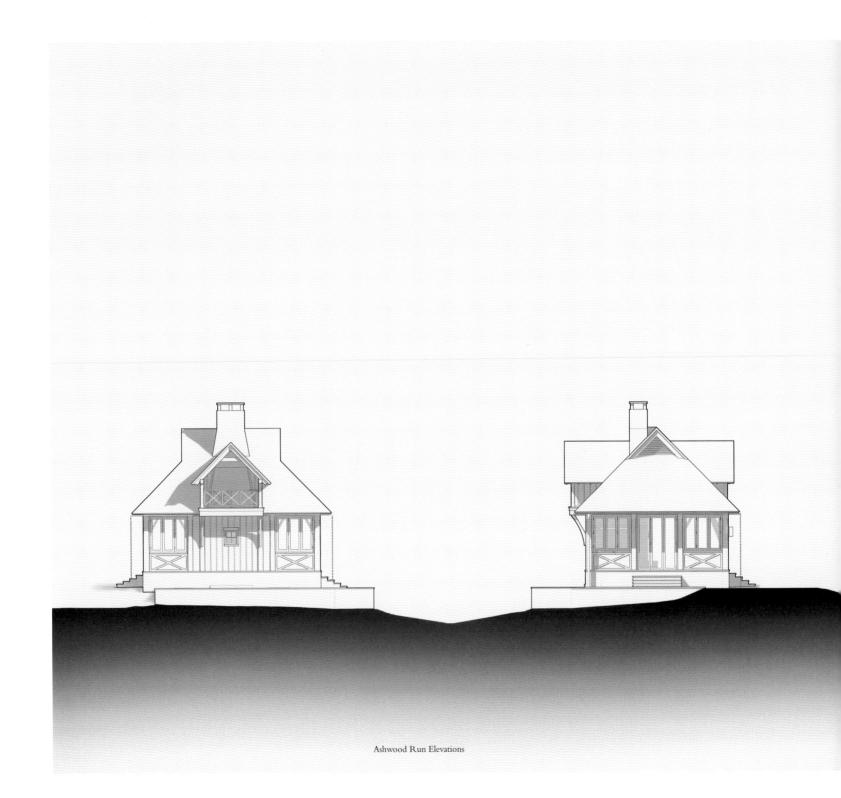

Ashwood Run Elevations

Ashwood Run Site Plan

Ashwood Run

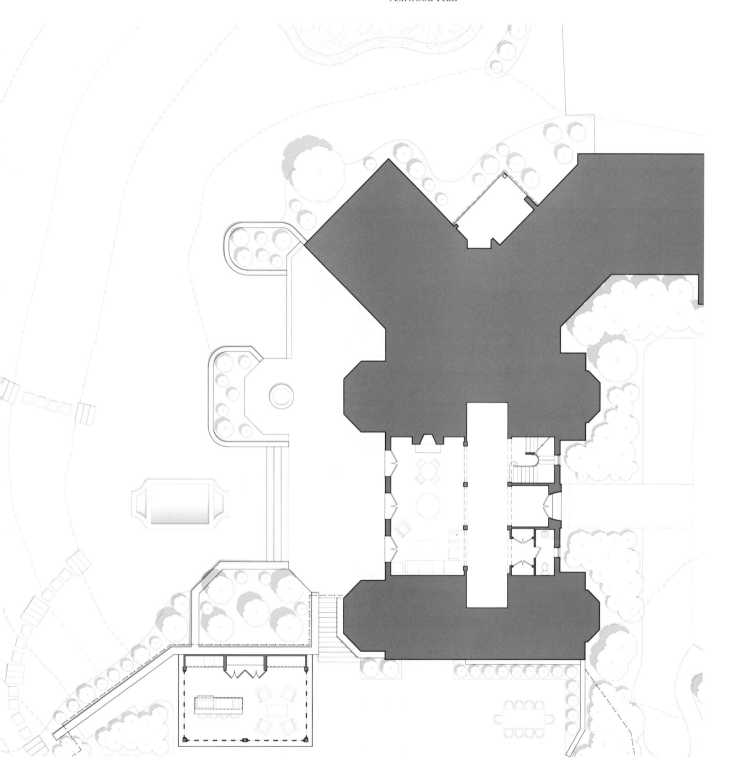

Ashwood Run

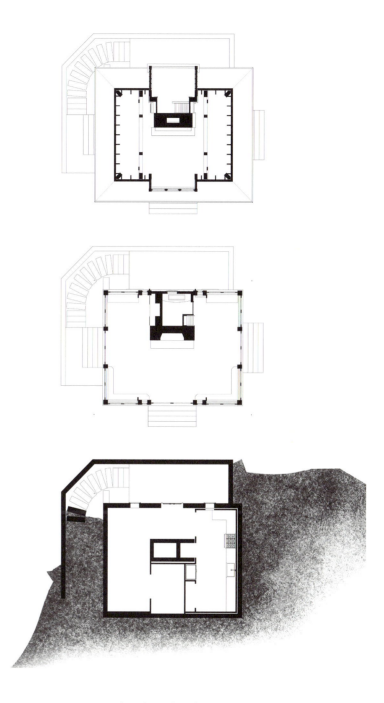

Ashwood Run Floor Plans

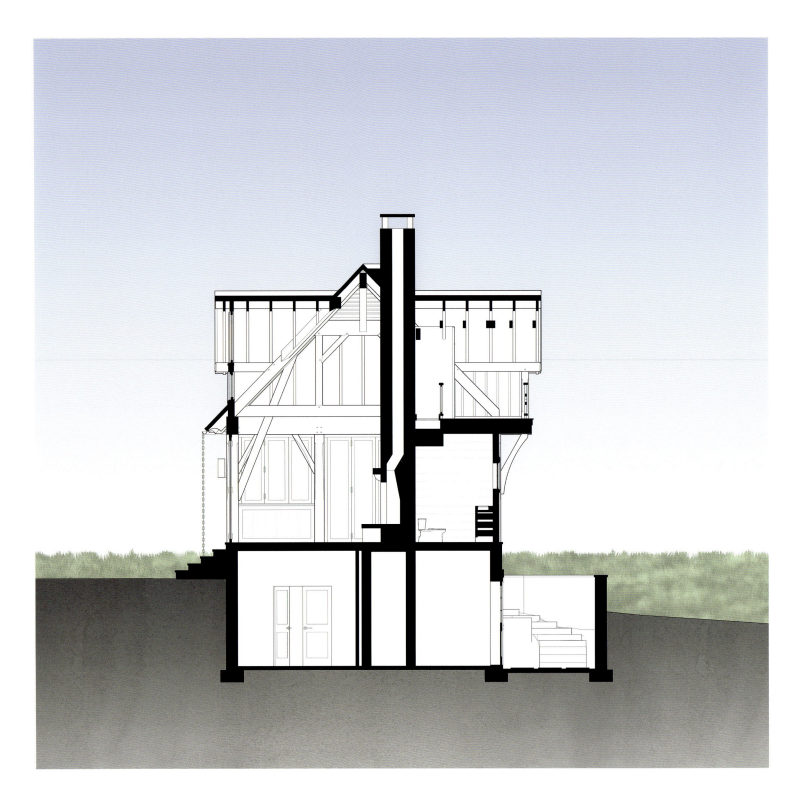

Ashwood Run

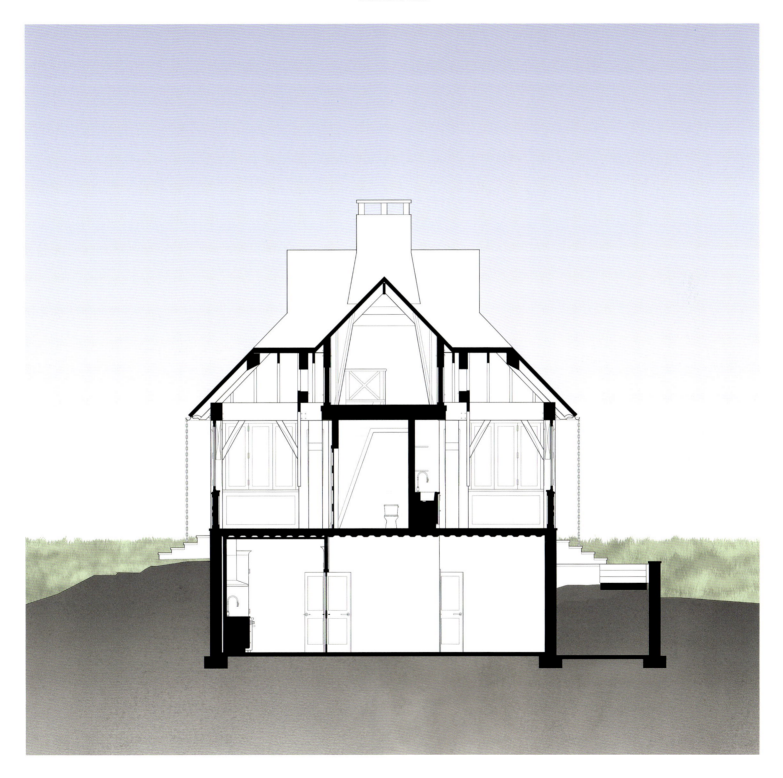

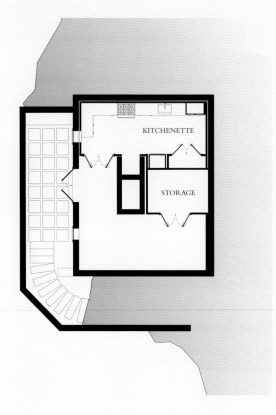
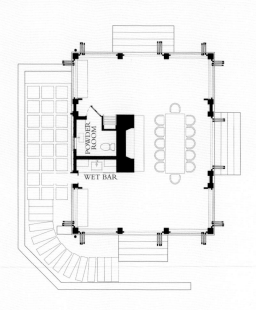
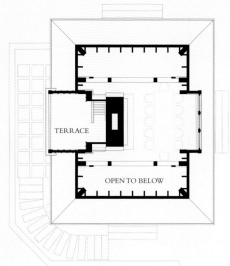
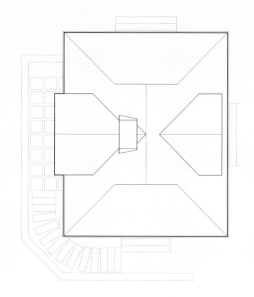

Ashwood Run Floor Plans

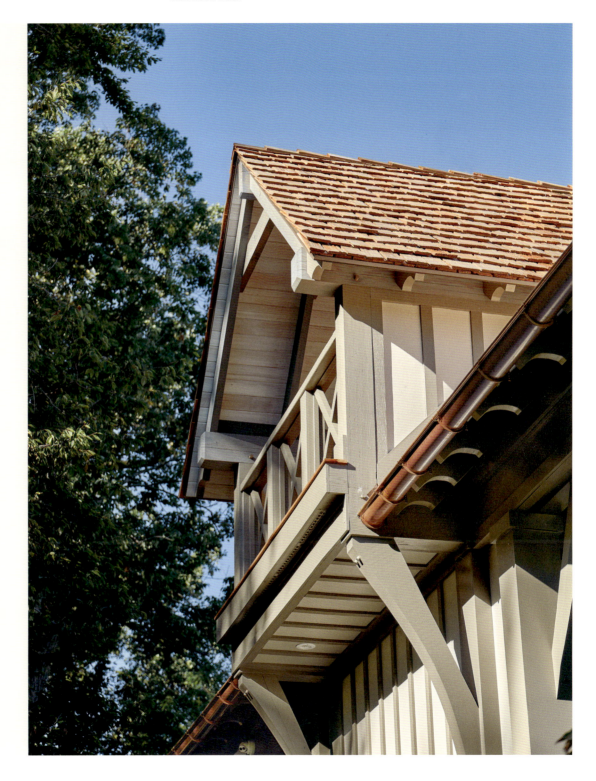

Ashwood Run

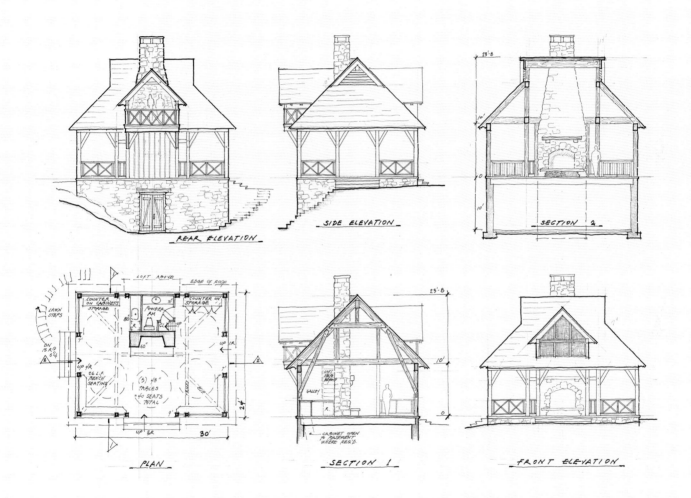

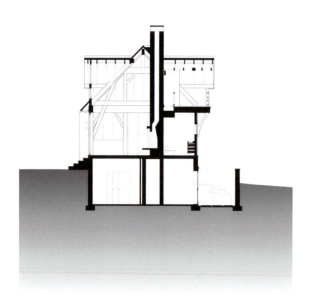

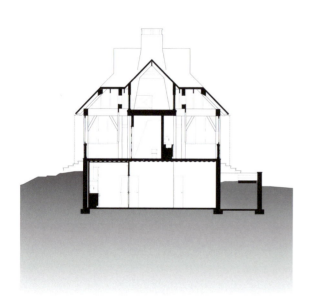

Ashwood Run Building Sections

Ashwood Run

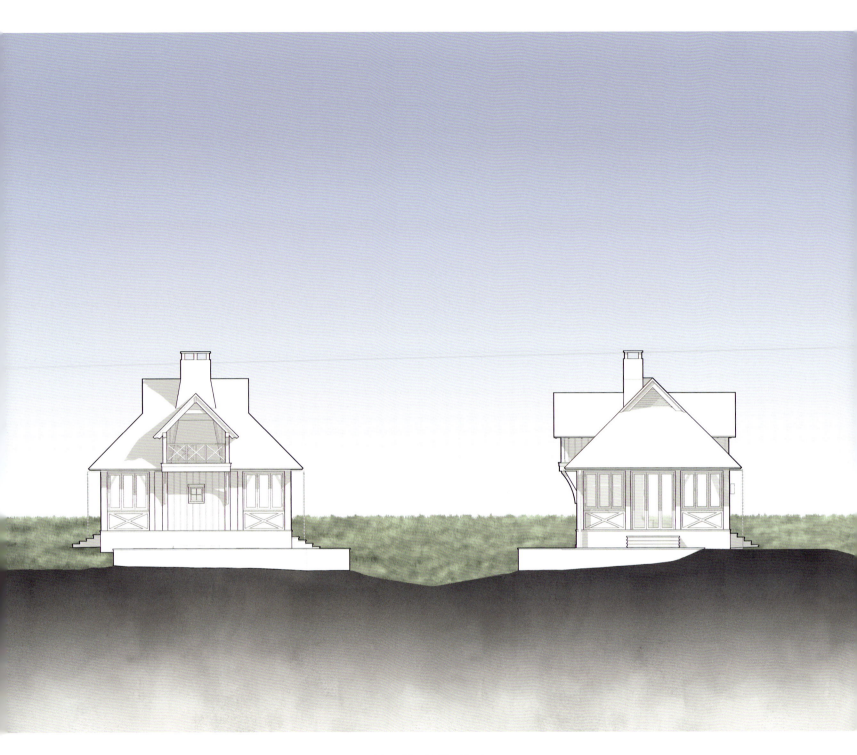

Ashwood Run Building Elevations

Ashwood Run

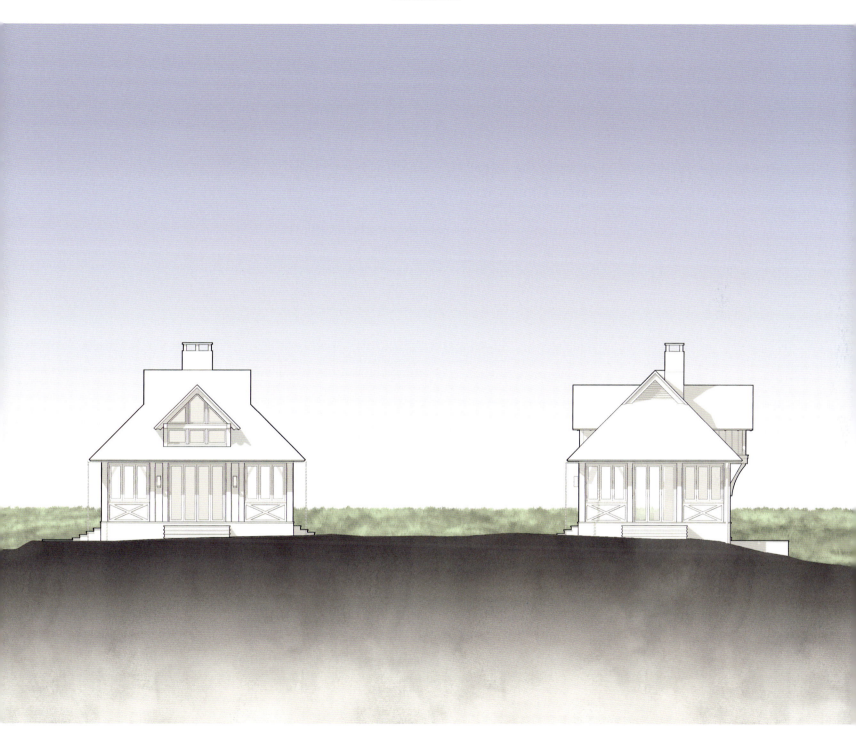

Ashwood Run Building Elevations

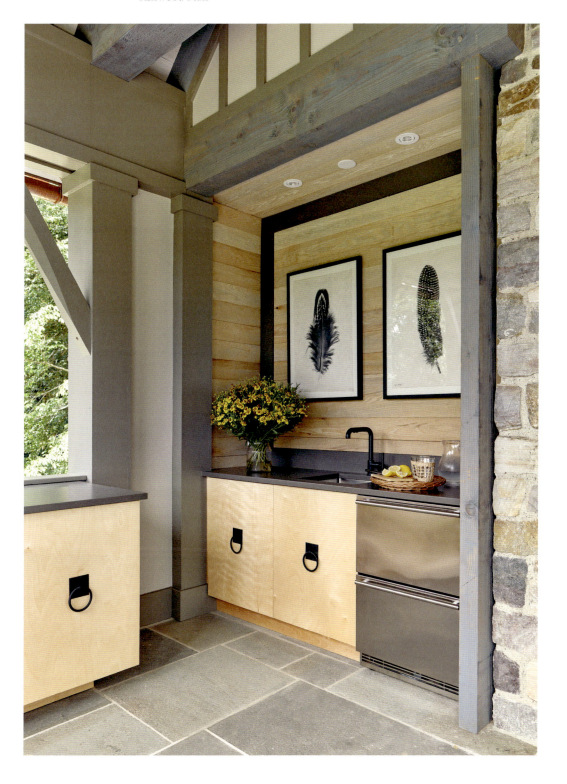

Ashwood Run

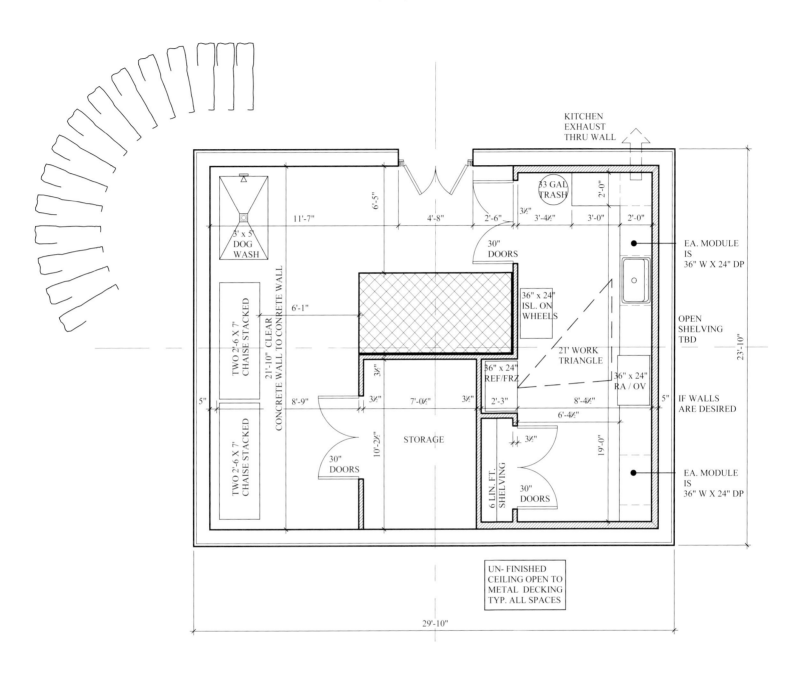

Basement Plan

Ashwood Run

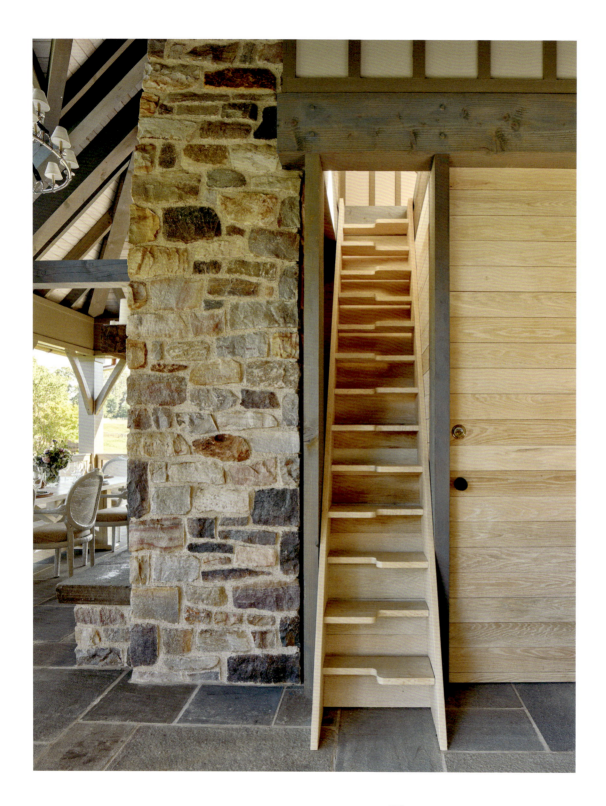

Ashwood Run

Ashwood Run

Ashwood Run

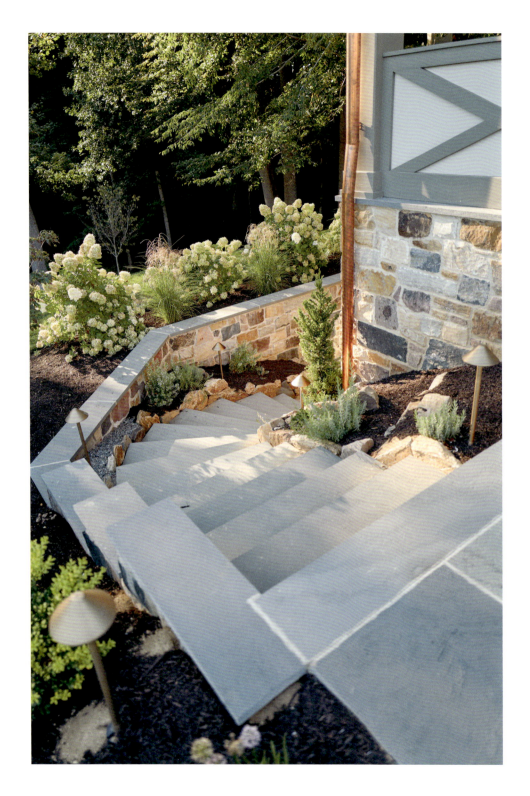

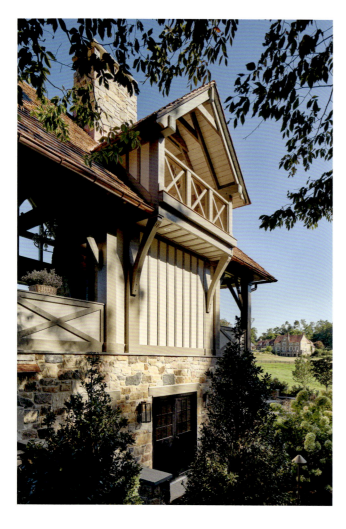

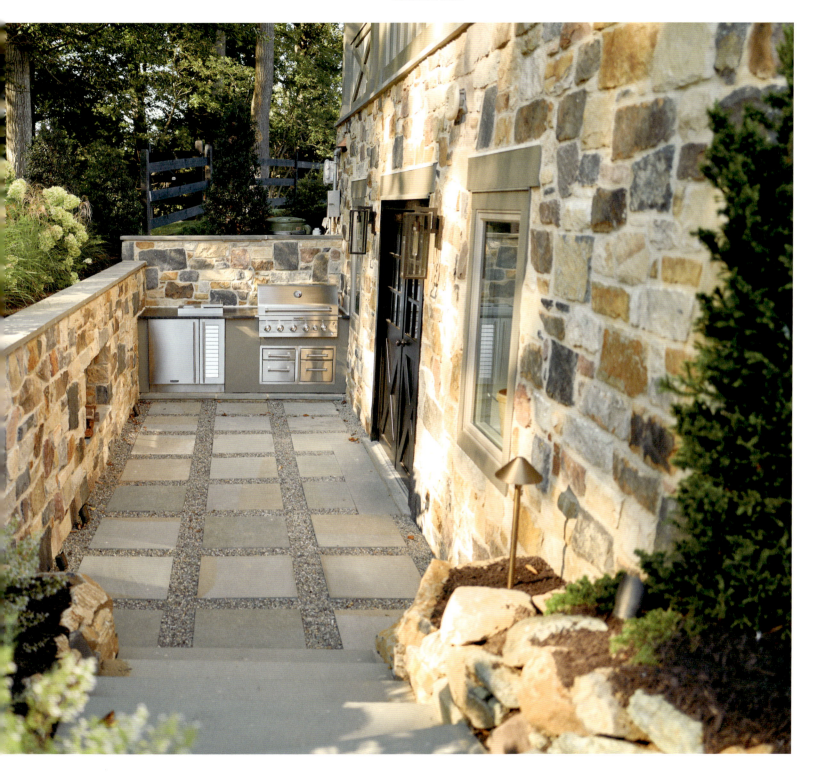

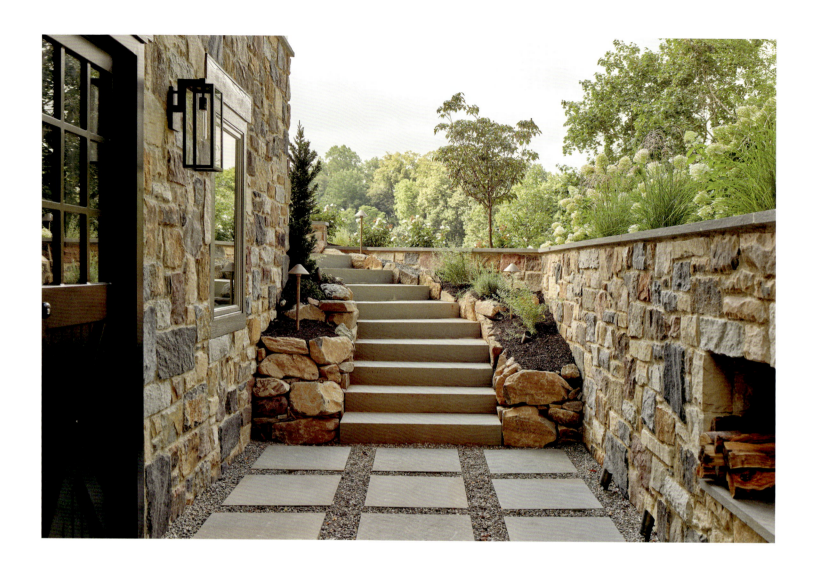

Ashwood Run

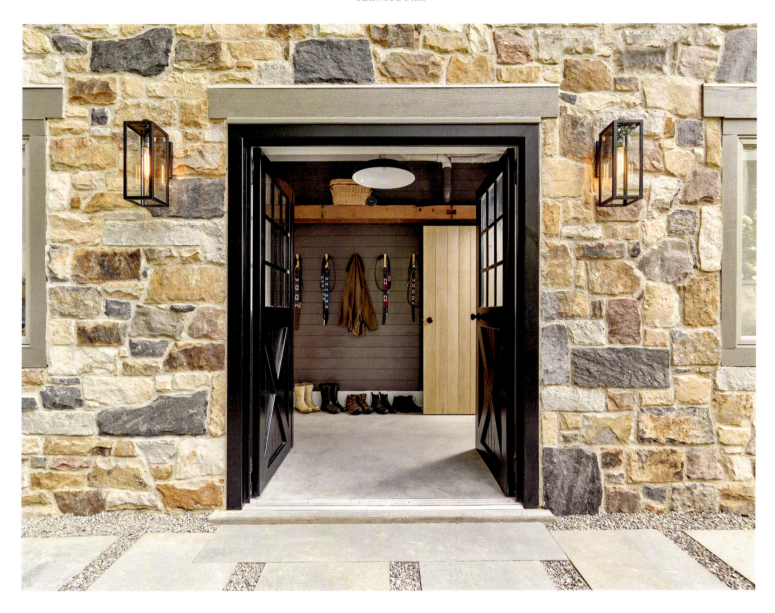

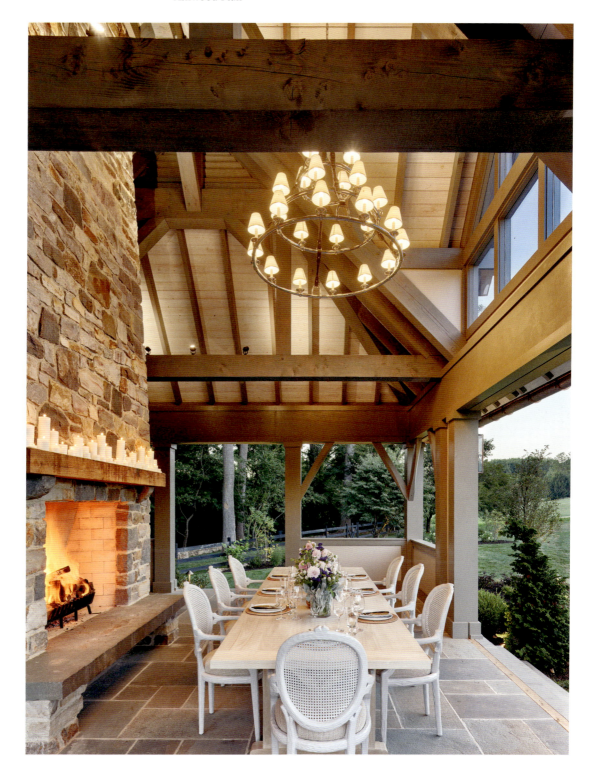

Ashwood Run

Construction

Ashwood Run

Ashwood Run Elevations

Ashwood Run

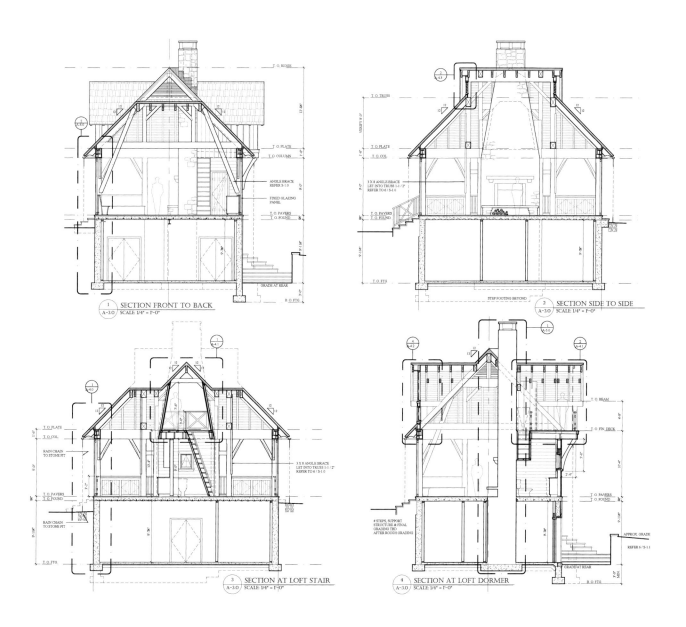

Ashwood Run Sections

Ashwood Run

Ashwood Run

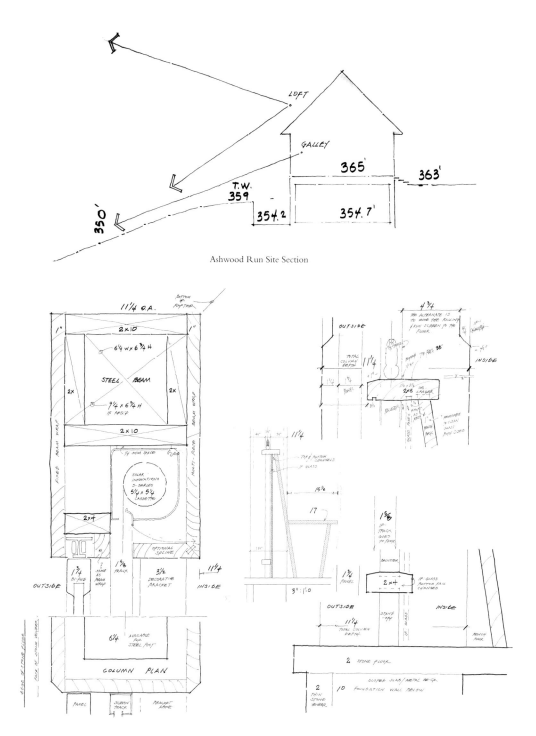

Ashwood Run Site Section

Ashwood Run Working Drawings

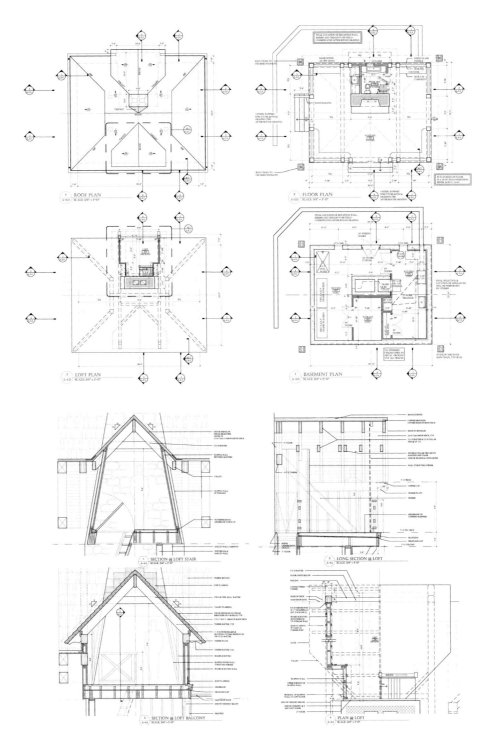

Ashwood Run Working Drawings

Ashwood Run

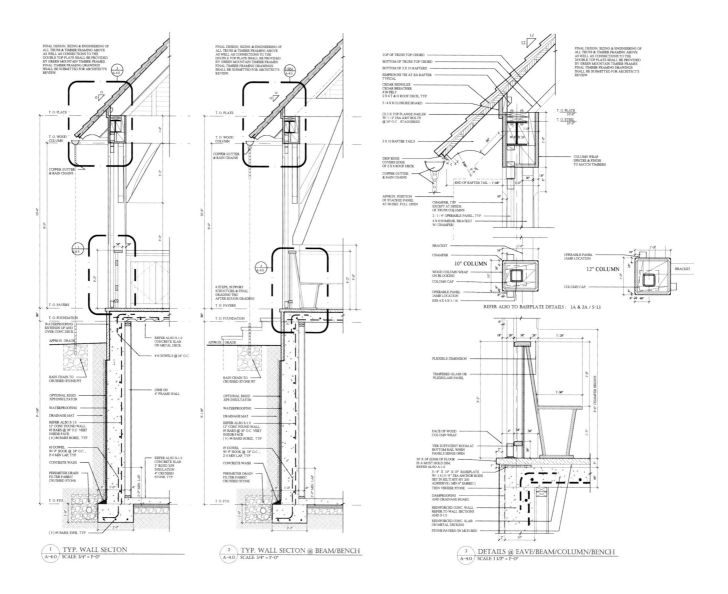

Ashwood Run Working Drawings

Ashwood Run

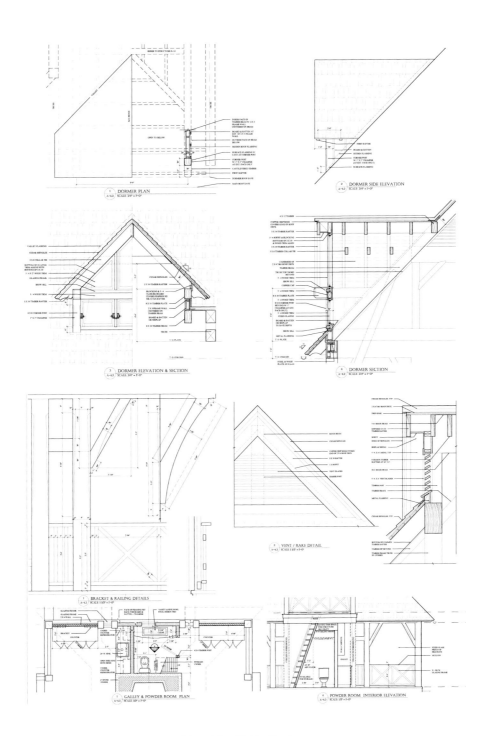

Ashwood Run Working Drawings

Ashwood Run

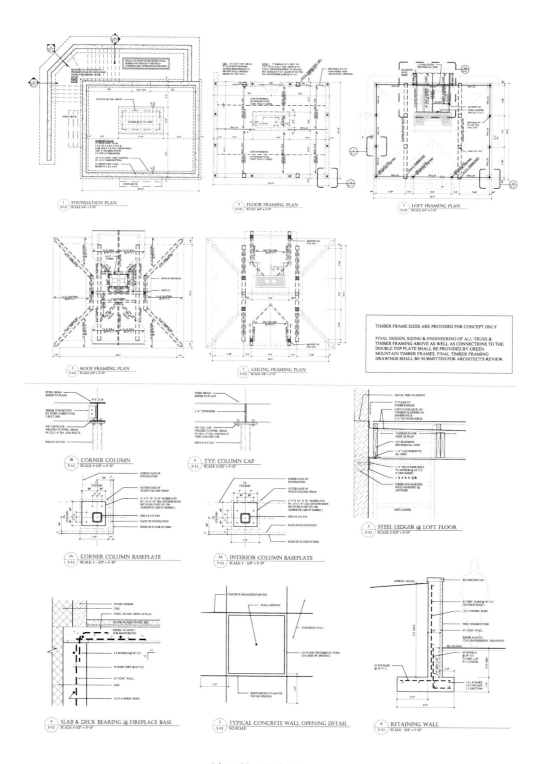

Ashwood Run Working Drawings

Ashwood Run

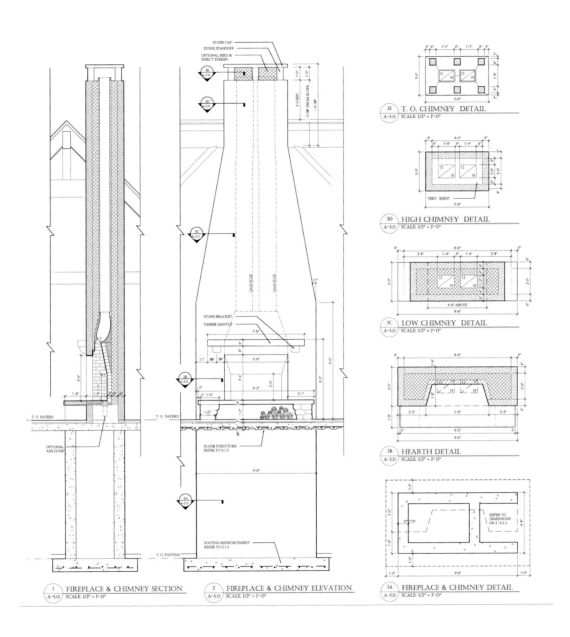

Ashwood Run Fireplace Working Drawings

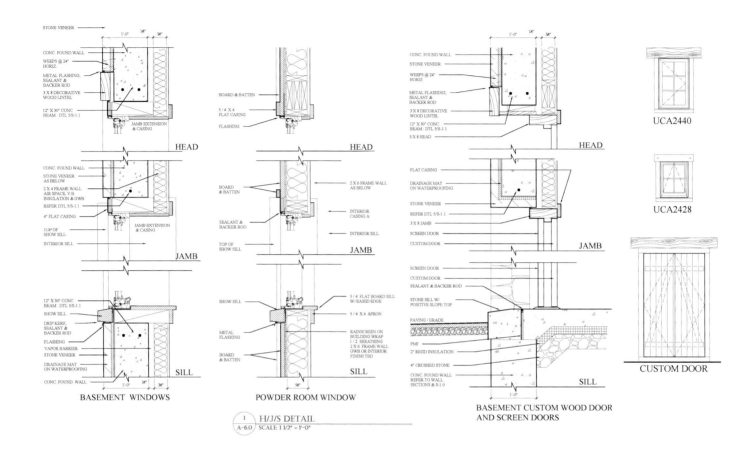

Ashwood Run

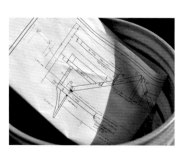

Ashwood Run

Ashwood Run

Ashwood Run

Concluding Thoughts

A Fireside Discussion
between Author and Patron

~

The company, then, were feasting in silence, as though at the command of some greater authority, when Philip the comedian knocked at the door and told the porter to announce who he was and why he desired to be admitted ... Philip, standing at the threshold of the men's hall where the banquet was served, announced: "You all know that I am a comedian; and so I've come here in the firm belief that it's funnier to come to your dinner uninvited than invited." "Well, then," said Callias, "take a seat; for the guests, though well fed, as you can see, on seriousness, are perhaps rather ill supplied with laughter." (Xenophon of Athens, *Symposium*, I, 11)

Victor Deupi – When we first discussed this project, you mentioned that you had lived in Italy as you began your career in finance in Milan. You briefly discuss this in your preface, but I was wondering if perhaps you could expand upon it further, describing your experiences in Italy and how that translated into a love of Italian culture, art, architecture, and ultimately well-being?

Julieann Shanahan – I traveled in Italy as much as I could afford to when I studied abroad and then returned there to work and study further. At the time, I was trying to absorb everything I could from an aesthetic perspective – the presentation of food, how fashion was tailored and, of course, architectural design. I was still quite young and impressionable. To this day I still give great pause to a remarkable triptych or the entrance way to a building.

I was very taken by how Italians translate beauty and incorporate it into their daily aaesthetic – which is so important to them and their culture. For Italians, it's not solely about the end result but the experience along the way – meaning, as they walk to work in the morning it is still important to look good and feel good. It is not about just arriving at the job. The Italians elegantly incorporate comfort, health, and happiness – along with looking good – to arrive at a state of well-being.

Well-being is a tricky concept for me because I tend to get overly focused on one project or task and forget about everything else. I must consciously make time and spaces to recharge, which is why creating these three pavilions thoughtfully became so important to me.

Victor Deupi – At the time, did you have any particular cities, towns, or landscapes in Italy that caught your attention? Are there any specific buildings that you recall?

Julieann Shanahan – I recall most vividly the rolling hills of Emilia Romagna, the *Navigli* section of Milan and the doors on the east façade of the Baptistry of the Duomo in Florence by Lorenzo Ghiberti – also known as the Gates of Paradise.

The first two recollections I mentioned engender an immediate sense of warmth. The rolling hills of Emilia Romagna present a level of comfort combining with Etruscan history and are similar to the topography where I now live. *Navigli* is just a great, often overlooked, area of Milan. It is such a cozy, canal-lined neighborhood in a tenaciously busy and cosmopolitan city. It is amazing during the holidays at year end when it is specially illuminated.

The Gates of Paradise consist of ten panels set in bronze that each tell a different story and took 21 years to create. It is the narrative and craftsmanship that keeps my attention. As you and I have previously discussed, the entry points are so important to a building or property because they set the stage of what is to come. That is why we returned to Peter Zimmerman to design the front gate and front doors of our home. The front doors took a fair amount of dialog to bring in more sunlight without using transom windows because of structural impediments. The front gates took on a life of their own adding cobblestone, widening the approach and customizing the actual gates with bleached oak that is used in the pavilions. Both entry points communicate themes of what you will see and feel at our home.

Victor Deupi – You recently returned from a trip to Sicily, Amalfi, and Rome. Did that trip change the way you see the project as it approaches its final stages?

Julieann Shanahan – On this last trip, the concept of patronage was revitalized and crystallized in my mind. We toured Palazzo

Barberini and were so impressed by the vast collection of artworks housed there by one family by incredible artists ranging from Filippo Lippi to Caravaggio. I really appreciated the amount of time and long-standing relationships it took to build their enormous, far-reaching collection.

When you first suggested the concept of patronage in the book title I wondered, "Is that what is really going on here?" We have employed the concept of collaboration in every project we have tackled which is so vitally important in a successful patron relationship. I truly enjoy the give and take of ideas and consider collaboration tantamount to patronage. Every detail of the pavilions was discussed to an extreme degree – from the truss design to the bleaching of the wood species and gutter materials to stone illumination – and numerous professionals were consulted. The same architect, general contractor, interior designer and landscape architect were used over a seven-year period and long-term relationships were fostered. I do not take their level of expertise and input for granted.

Victor Deupi – Of course the Barberinis were great patrons of art and architecture, a papal family of extraordinary influence. But you can also be a patron at a much smaller scale, like Alvise Cornaro who I mentioned at the beginning of the Introduction to this book. And while yes, his family had Venetian Doges, he was a much more modest individual. I see the Loggia and Odeon in his backyard not unlike the two pavilions around your pool, at least in terms of their spatial organization, and to a certain extent use, for instance in dining and conversation. If his memoir is correct and he lived to be a hundred years old, then perhaps through your building efforts you will as well. Wouldn't that be nice?

Julieann Shanahan – Yes, it most definitely would. We want the buildings to be meaningful and relevant not just today, but also in a long period of time from now. Intentionally, we crafted the buildings to be timeless and hardy – to withstand the seasonal temperature changes, create a backdrop for enjoyment and set the stage for a positive mood or affectation. We also want them to be low maintenance and not fussy in any way – which should extend their lifetimes.

Victor Deupi – England has also played an important part in shaping your vision of art and design. You often travel there, and you live in a region of Philadelphia, the Main Line, that is known for its English inspired historic houses. There are not that many Mediterranean Revival houses in the region. Do you see a relationship between England and Italy?

Julieann Shanahan – Both the English and Italians have taken older countryside homes and renovated with spartan modern interiors that I have tried to imitate here. Of course, not everyone does this in England and Italy while renovating older homes, but those who have done so have greatly inspired me.

In some cases, the English and Italians tend to go to even more extremes than what I did – taking a home that was built in previous centuries and contrasting it with an unquestionable modern aesthetic of today. From a design perspective, they both do such a great job restoring exteriors and incorporating minimalist interiors resulting in an understated elegance in the juxtaposition. This type of renovation of mixing historical and contemporary elements can be found in many other places as well, but Italy and England are the two that I am drawn to over and over and have now become so familiar to me.

In terms of the pavilions, the Italian courtyard influence is apparent in the pool pavilion and cabana orientations that work together to

Concluding Thoughts

nestle the pool and create privacy. In our third pavilion, the English influence is present in the modern interpretation of the barn and the details – for example, the widow's walk staircase to the loft is English influenced. We stayed in a treehouse in England where they used that style of staircase.

Victor Deupi – Even though you live in a Cotswold style country house, you tend to shy away from the term traditional. In fact, the interiors of your house are, dare I say, audacious. I had tried to say that in my text, but you were reluctant to use the term as you felt it could be interpreted in a pejorative sense. However, I see it as bold and daring, which is what we used instead. So, how do you see these two aspects of architecture and design working together?

Julieann Shanahan – I have struggled with this concept endlessly of where the things I have worked on neatly fit in a traditional, transitional, modern, or contemporary framework. I am so conscious of symmetry which I view as necessary for creating harmony, and ultimately sets the stage for an environment that fosters comfort and well-being. Along with symmetry, I have a high adherence to functionality and utility, which is one of the many reasons the renovations I work on take a long time. But I get fearful around the traditional genre because I don't want to redo what has been done before repeatedly. This is not meant to be a criticism; it is just where I am the most comfortable. Isn't that what design is ultimately about? Finding a sense of comfort at home.

My intent is to take inspiration from historical architecture and design and then build upon it. I want to look through a contemporary lens to reflect how I will best use things today in my family's daily lives and how that can be adapted easily as life changes. That is how I try to marry the traditional Cotswold influence – which fits the setting well – with modern design and my experiences.

Victor Deupi – You have three children, and now you have three pavilions. They are offspring of sorts. How do you see the three (pavilions) and how do you like to experience them, either alone or with the family, husband and dogs included?

Julieann Shanahan – Like my children, I see the buildings individually, since we built them one at a time and they serve unique purposes, and collectively, since they all celebrate being outdoors.

All three buildings are defined spaces where I am not distracted by the stack of things to do or catch up on. The buildings are definitely meant for relaxation, to read a book or listen to nature but you can go there alone and get work done as well or host a meeting. Intentionally, all three pavilions foster a new, separate and distinct environment to minimize distractions without leaving home. Usually, we use the buildings to congregate after swimming, or to read or eat – which includes hanging out after s'mores! There is an automatic reset button when you enter and exit all of the buildings.

But now that I think about it, the most subtle use I did not anticipate for all three buildings is the interplay of light—either light emanating from the buildings or how the buildings capture light. Granted the two pool pavilions were built to create shade from the sun, but after the sun sets we can put all of the lights on in the buildings to view them from the house. You can also see the buildings illuminated from the street even though they are set back a fair distance. In this scenario, they truly do look like enchanting garden houses on the horizon. As the winter sun hangs lower in the sky, it still manages to warm the pavilions. They are also heated so you can have dinner in the building with the feeling you are in a toasty greenhouse even in November.

Victor Deupi – Do your husband or children have a preference … what about the dogs, they have a particularly notable space in the third pavilion?

Julieann Shanahan – I don't think we could pick one pavilion objectively, but Ashwood is the newest and has a sense of novelty. As I mentioned in the preface, my family had serious renovation fatigue before we started the last pavilion, Ashwood Run. So, I really tried to consider how they would enjoy the building in the creation and construction process. In terms of cooking, Ashwood has a catering kitchen and a smoker that you don't have to monitor every minute or few hours so that pleases my husband to no end. The lookout loft is the playhouse that my children never had and also a place where adults can go to

feel like a kid again. My son really wanted a wood burning fireplace, so the fieldstone fireplace is the main focal point of the building. Additionally, there is a firepit right outside of Ashwood where you can view its exterior from another perspective. We have two very large dogs so we made a very grand dog shower – that humans could use if need be – in the basement across from the kitchen. Ashwood emanates additional soft light with gas lanterns at the front entrance that we can see from our home as we eat dinner in the kitchen.

Victor Deupi – Wow, usually dogs get to use our showers, how delightful it would be to be able to use one of theirs … but I digress. So, how did you decide to work with Peter Zimmerman Architects, and what aspects of the office or portfolio fit in well with your vision?

Prospector, Peter Zimmerman. Photography by Audrey Hall. (Above and following page)

Concluding Thoughts

Mill Creek Terrace, Peter Zimmerman.
Photo courtesy of Tom Crane.

Julieann Shanahan – I interviewed several architects and Peter was clear that he was up for the job. I was struck by the range of projects he was capable of doing both locally and nationwide. Specifically, I was drawn to a project he did in Miami— the Setai Penthouse project in South Beach that was a contrast to local projects and demonstrated his range of ability. Another great example of Peter's work is a very modern home in Idaho named Prospector, that has been widely acclaimed and uses many of the same materials that we have used at my home.

Obviously, Peter's enormous experience over roughly 40 years was very convincing. He taught me so much about delineating spaces visually, sound wise and use wise. I should also add that he displayed great flexibility when I kept adding to the scope of the initial main house renovation and to the list of uses for the pavilions. Both lists kept mushrooming to a considerable extent.

Victor Deupi – This is your first book with Oscar Riera Ojeda, and my fifth. How did you decide to work with him and his team? What were some of his publications that caught your attention?

Julieann Shanahan – First and foremost, is Oscar's view of the details and where he brings the eye in a photo or the storyline of a book. He highlights the things that I, and others, want to see and, quite frankly, everyone should notice.

I was doing research for the Ashwood design that was leaning towards a barn influenced pavilion and found Oscar's works. I started with the *Figueras Polo Stables* and *Bank Barn*. The *Figueras Polo Stables* uses light in a stunning fashion with glass, wood, and against concrete with even a reflecting pool/drinking source for horses. It also makes use of the horizon line of the Pampa in Argentina so well, but that does not lend itself to the topography here in Pennsylvania. Then I went to *Bank Barn*, which is essentially a wood and glass barn style home with a metal seamed roof built into the side of a hill in Vermont. That does fit better with the local topography where I live. But I would not have been able to obtain permits to disturb the slopes towards our woodlands in the back of the house. So, we moved off the slope and made a stone retaining wall that we use as a tiny – it is only eight feet wide – courtyard.

The commonality of these two books is the artistry of mixing textures, which is so vitally important to me to keep my interest. I don't like clutter or excessive adornment but mixing the warmth of wood with the hardness of concrete and stone keeps me interested. That is why I was eventually drawn to *Stables, High Design for Horse and Home*, the book that you and Oscar worked on together. The craftsmanship of the stonework in the Stables book, especially in Mexico, is incredibly spectacular. The complex

Concluding Thoughts

Birdseye, Bank Barn.

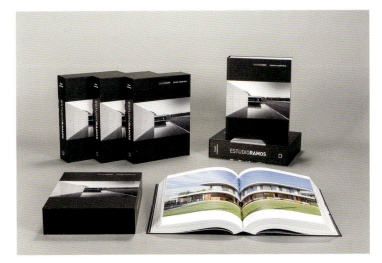

Estudio Ramos, Honest Modernism.

mixing of materials in one space or room that can occur in barns and pavilions isn't something everyone has the opportunity to do in their own homes. We were able to mix materials in all our pavilions to create an inner warmth within them.

In addition to Oscar's specific subject or project books, I am captivated by his compilations of work by a singular architect such as *Hutker Architects' Heirlooms to Live In* and Estudio Ramos' *Honest Modernism* which range design wise from northeastern United States vernacular to Argentinian modern. I prefer to do research across different geographic regions – whether it is around the world or across the nation – to see what works well elsewhere and could be assimilated at home design-wise through a contemporary lens. Books have the power to take you to different places on a deep level in one design meeting and provide unique content

Hutker Architects, Heirlooms to Live In.

287

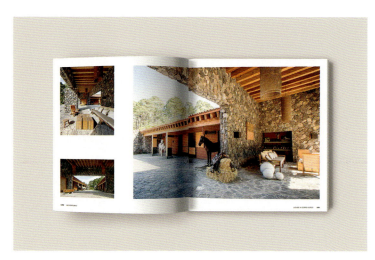

Stables, High Design for Horse and Home, Rizzoli.

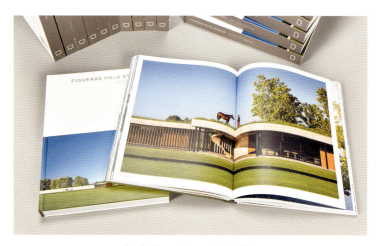

Estudio Ramos, Figueras Polo Stables.

that you cannot cover otherwise. It is not the same as a magazine article or Pinterest.

Victor Deupi – This has been great Julieann, not just seeing the pavilions evolve, but also the process of writing this book with you and Oscar. I often say that I write books to help me sort out my thinking, and this book has clarified several issues I've thought about but never quite found a way to articulate. This certainly has been in the words of Amor Towles, a favorite novelist of mine, a one-of-a-kind kind of book, which brings me to my final question. Leon Battista Alberti's personal emblem was a winged eye with lightning bolts and the Latin term *quid tum* (what next) written underneath ... so, I ask you Julieann, *quid tum*?

Julieann Shanahan – Oh that is a tough one! In totality, renovating our home, constructing the three pavilions, and restoring the gardens took seven years. But I am still accumulating ideas and inspirations, much to my chagrin. At home, I am going to do a cobblestone area by our garages to create a courtyard – a recurring theme at our house – and maybe a fieldstone geometric sculpture in the back woodlands. We also are inclined to build somewhere; it is just a matter of finding the right location and enticing our children to visit as they get older!

I am so glad you found this to be a one-of-a-kind kind of book, given all of your experience. So what is next for you?

Victor Deupi – As for me, the writing never stops. I hope that in your case, building never ceases either!

Appendix

Dams, Bernd H., and Andrew Zega. *Pleasure Pavilions and Follies in the Gardens of the Ancien Régime*. Paris and New York: Flammarion, 1995.

Dodds, George. *Building Desire: on the Barcelona Pavilion*. New York: Routledge, 2005.

Eusebius. *Life of Constantine*. Translated with an Introduction by Averil Cameron and Stuart Hall. Oxford: Clarendon Press, 1999.

Fielding, Mantle. *Dictionary of American Painters, Sculptors and Engravers*. Edited by Genevieve C. Doran. Greens Farms, Conn.: Modern Books and Crafts, 1974.

Fiocco, Giuseppe. *Alvise Cornaro il suo tempo e le sue opere*. Venice: Neri Pozza Editore, 1965.

Hersey, George L. *Architecture, Poetry, and Number in the Royal Palace at Caserta*. Cambridge, Mass: MIT Press, 1983.

Historia Augusta, Volume II: Caracalla. Geta. Opellius Macrinus. Diadumenianus. Elagabalus. Severus Alexander. The Two Maximini. The Three Gordians. Maximus and Balbinus. Translated by David Magie. Cambridge, Mass.: Harvard University Press (Loeb Classical Library), 1924.

Irwin, Robert. *The Alhambra*. Cambridge, Mass.: Harvard University Press, 2004.

Jordan, John W. *A History of Delaware County, Pennsylvania, and Its People*. 2 Vols. New York: Lewis Historical Publishing Company, 1914.

Kathrens, Michael C. *American Splendor: The Residential Architecture of Horace Trumbauer*. New York: Acanthus Press, 2002.

McNeil, Collin F. *Bright Hunting Morn: The 125th Anniversary of the Radnor Hunt*. New York: The Derrydale Press, 2009.

Morris, Edwin T. *The Gardens of China: History, Art, and Meanings*. New York: Scribner, 1983.

Mott, George, and Sally Sample Aall. *Follies and Pleasure Pavilions: England, Ireland, Scotland, Wales*. New York: Harry N. Abrams, 1989.

Necipoglu, Gülru. *Architecture, Ceremonial, and Power: The Topkapi Palace in the Fifteenth and Sixteenth Centuries*. Cambridge, Mass.: MIT Press, 1991.

Palladio, Andrea. *The Four Books on Architecture*. Translated by Robert Tavernor and Richard Schofield. Cambridge, Mass., and London: The MIT Press, 2001.

Pliny the Younger. *Letters,* Volume I: Books 1-7. Translated by Betty Radice. Cambridge, Mass.: Harvard University Press (Loeb Classical Library), 1969.

Polybius. *The Histories*, Volume I: Books 1-2. Translated by W. R. Paton. Revised by F. W. Walbank, Christian Habicht. Cambridge, Mass.: Harvard University Press (Loeb Classical Library), 2010.

Ran, Wei. *Buddhist Buildings: The Architecture of Monasteries, Pagodas, and Stone Caves*. New York: CN Times Books, 2014.

Rich, Anthony. *A Dictionary of Roman and Greek Antiquities*. London: Longmans, 1890.

Rykwert, Joseph. "House and Home." *Social Research 58* (Spring 1991): 51–62.

Rykwert, Joseph. *The Villa: from Ancient to Modern*. New York: H.N. Abrams, 2000.

Samson, Miles David. *Hut Pavilion Shrine: Architectural Archetypes in Mid-Century Modernism*. Farnham, Surrey and Burlington, VT: Ashgate, 2015.

Sancho, José Luis. *La arquitectura de los sitios reales: catálogo histórico de los palacios, jardines y patronatos reales del Patrimonio Nacional*. Madrid: Patrimonio Nacional, 1995.

Schafer, Gil. *A Place to Call Home: Tradition, Style, and Memory in the New American House*. New York: Rizzoli, 2017.

Scott, Janny. *The Beneficiary: Fortune, Misfortune, and the Story of My Father*. New York: Riverhead Books, 2019.

Semenzato, C. ed., "Trattato di architettura," in *Trattati*. Milan: Edizioni Il Polifilo, 1985,

Serlio, Sebastiano. *Sebastiano Serlio on Architecture*. Translated by Vaughan Hart and Peter Hicks. New Haven: Yale University Press, 2001.

Smith, George. *History of Delaware County, Pennsylvania from the Discovery of the Territory Included Within its Limits to the Present Time: With a Notice of the Geology of the County, and Catalogues of its Minerals, Plants, Quadrupeds and Birds*. Philadelphia: H.B. Ashmead, 1862.

Tavernor, Robert. *Palladio and Palladianism*. London: Thames & Hudson, 2003.

Vitruvius M. Pollio, *De Architectura*. Translated by Frank Granger. Cambridge, Mass.: Harvard University Press (The Loeb Classical Library), 1931.

Weaver, Lawrence. "Ardenrun Place." *Country Life*. January 21, 1911, 90-96.

Wilber, Donald Newton. *Persian Gardens and Garden Pavilions*. Washington, DC: Dumbarton Oaks, 1979.

Wiley, Samuel T., and Winfield Scott Garner. *Biographical and Historical Cyclopedia of Delaware County, Penn.: Comprising a Historical Sketch of the County*. Richmond, IN: Gresham Pub. Co., 1894.

Wilson Jones, Mark. *Principles of Roman Architecture*. New Haven, Conn.: Yale University Press, 2000.

Wren, David Nelson. *Ardrossan: The Last Great Estate on the Philadelphia Main Line*. New York: Bauer and Dean Publishers, 2018.

Xenophon. *Memorabilia, Oeconomicus, Symposium, Apology*. Translated by E.C. Marchant and O.J. Todd. Cambridge, Mass.: Harvard University Press (The Loeb Classical Library), 1914.

Yun, Qiao, et al. *Ancient Chinese Architecture*. Hong Kong and Beijing: Joint Publishing Company and the China Building Industry Press, 1982.

Project Credits

House
Size: 8.000 sq ft
Design: 1998
Renovations: 2016 - 2020

Pool Pavilion
Size: 500 sq ft
Design: 2016
Completion: 2018

Pool Cabana
Size: 250 sq ft
Design: 2017
Completion: 2019

Ashwood Run
Size: 750 sq ft
Design: 2020
Completion: 2022

Architectural Design
Peter Zimmerman
Peter Zimmerman
Architects

Principal in Charge
Tyson Chamberlain
Chris Hoffman

Architecture Illustrations
Max Bliss
Michael J. Farkas

Interior Design
Robin Willis
Robin Willis Interiors

Builder and General Contractor
David Soto
Soto Construction, LLC

Photography
All photographs by Jeffrey Totaro, Architectural Photographer, except for those on pages 196, 197 and 250, which are by Brian Lauer; and those credited under each photograph.

Historical Archivist
Phil Graham
Publishing and Graphics

Landscape Architect
David Gaffney
Landscaping by Gaffney, Inc.

Civil Engineer
Nicholas L. Vastardis
Vastardis Consulting
Engineers, LLC

Structural Engineer
Bradford R. Oliver
The Kachele Group, Inc.

Timber Engineer
Bruce March
Green Mountain Timber
Frames, Inc

Building Inspector
Radnor Township

Acknowledgements

With special gratitude to the Radnor Historical Society and the
Montgomery-Scott-Wheeler family for providing the context
to make this project so exceptional. Also, endless thanks to David Soto
and Robin Willis. We could not have achieved all that we did
with any other contractor or design team. Finally, profound gratitude to my
husband, Keven, who exhibited unwavering support and flexibility,
even when it was not easy or convenient to do so.